TAX REFORM IN

EIGHTEENTH CENTURY LOMBARDY

DANIEL M. KLANG

EAST EUROPEAN QUARTERLY, BOULDER
DISTRIBUTED BY COLUMBIA UNIVERSITY PRESS
NEW YORK

1977

EAST EUROPEAN MONOGRAPHS, NO. XXVII

Daniel M. Klang is Associate Professor of History
at the University of British Columbia

Printed in the United States of America

The book has been published with the help of a grant from the
Social Science Research Council of Canada, using funds provided by
the Canada Council

EAST EUROPEAN MONOGRAPHS

The *East European Monographs* comprise scholarly books on the history and civilization of Eastern Europe. They are published by the *East European Quarterly* in the belief that these studies contribute substantially to the knowledge of the area and serve to stimulate scholarship and research.

1. *Political Ideas and the Enlightenment in the Romanian Principalities, 1750-1831.* By Vlad Georgescu. 1971.
2. *America, Italy and the Birth of Yugoslavia, 1917-1919.* By Dragan R. Zivojinovic. 1972.
3. *Jewish Nobles and Geniuses in Modern Hungary.* By William O. McCagg, Jr. 1972.
4. *Mixail Soloxov in Yugoslavia: Reception and Literary Impact.* By Robert F. Price. 1973.
5. *The Historical and Nationalist Thought of Nicolae Iorga.* By William O. Oldson, 1973.
6. *Guide to Polish Libraries and Archives.* By Richard C. Lewanski. 1974.
7. *Vienna Broadcasts to Slovakia, 1938-1939: A Case Study in Subversion.* By Henry Delfiner. 1974.
8. *The 1917 Revolution in Latvia.* By Andrew Ezergailis. 1974.
9. *The Ukraine in the United Nations Organization: A Study in Soviet Foreign Policy, 1944-1950.* By Konstantin Sawczuk. 1975.
10. *The Bosnian Church: A New Interpretation.* By John V. A. Fine, Jr. 1975.
11. *Intellectual and Social Developments in the Habsburg Empire from Maria Theresa to World War I.* Edited by Stanley B. Winters and Joseph Held. 1975.
12. *Ljudevit Gaj and the Illyrian Movement.* By Elinor Murray Despalatovic. 1975.
13. *Tolerance and Movements of Religious Dissent in Eastern Europe.* Edited by Bela K. Kiraly. 1975.
14. *The Parish Republic: Hlinka's Slovak People's Party, 1939-1945.* By Yeshayahu Jelinek. 1976.
15. *The Russian Annexation of Bessarabia, 1774-1828.* By George F. Jewsbury. 1976.
16. *Modern Hungarian Historiography.* By Steven Bela Vardy. 1976.
17. *Values and Community in Multi-National Yugoslavia.* By Gary K. Bertsch. 1976.
18. *The Greek Socialist Movement and the First World War: The Road to Unity.* By George B. Leon. 1976.
19. *The Radical Left in the Hungarian Revolution of 1848.* By Laszlo Deme. 1976.
20. *Hungary between Wilson and Lenin: The Hungarian Revolution of 1918-1919 and the Big Three.* By Peter Pastor. 1976.
21. *The Crises of France's East-Central European Diplomacy, 1933-1938.* By Anthony J. Komjathy. 1976.
22. *Polish Politics and National Reform, 1775-1788 .* By Daniel Stone. 1976.
23. *The Habsburg Empire in World War I.* Robert A. Kann, Bela K. Kiraly, and Paula S. Fichtner, eds. 1977.
24. *The Slovenes and Yugoslavism, 1890-1914.* By Carole Rogel. 1977.
25. *German-Hungarian Relations and the Swabian Problem.* By Thomas Spira. 1977.
26. *The Metamorphosis of a Social Class in Hungary during the Reign of Young Franz Joseph.* By Peter I. Hidas. 1977.
27. *Tax Reform in Eighteenth-Century Lombardy.* By Daniel M. Klang. 1977.

TABLE OF CONTENTS

INTRODUCTION 1
I. EARLY WORK ON THE TAX (1706-1733) 4
II. POMPEO NERI 24
III. COMPLETION OF THE TAX (1749-1758) 33
IV. THE REFORM OF LOCAL GOVERNMENT 45
V. THE TAX IN OPERATION 66
CONCLUSION 81
NOTES 83
BIBLIOGRAPHY 101
INDEX 108

INTRODUCTION

In the year 1760 the Austrian government completed and instituted a remarkable tax reform in its province of Lombardy. Involving careful measurement and evaluation of the land, as well as the renewal of local administration, the *Censimento* drew warm praise from Adam Smith for being exceptionally accurate.(1) At home in Milan an enthusiastic official compared the legislation, "the greatest work ever done in Europe," to the twelve tables of Roman law.(2) Indeed by 1791 its prestige was so great that the one-time center of opposition against it, the Congregation of State, an assembly of provincial and metropolitan advocates, now begged the crown not to make the slightest change in its operation.(3) During the next century Carlo Cattaneo, a notorious enemy of the Austrians, spoke of the land tax as a decisive instrument of agricultural progress, and its political practices on the communal and provincial level as superior to anything offered by Piedmontese unification.(4) In the 1880s a notable Italian scholar argued that the Censimento began a new era in the history of modern finance, and still today, two centuries after its completion, it is generally considered as the major achievement of Austrian rule in Lombardy.(5) Further to underline the importance of this great innovation one need only add that it was part of the process which allowed Italy, of all Mediterranean nations, to industrialize in the 19th century and escape, at least in some measure, from the endemic poverty of its geographic region.(6)

Naturally the Censimento has attracted the attention of historians, general accounts of 18th century Italy or Lombardy invariably touching upon it, often with great insight and mastery. Yet no modern study exists of its entire course from 1719 to 1760, and only a few works focus on some one of its phases or aspects.(7) This neglect is doubly unfortunate because the relevance of the subject extends beyond the immediate locality to all Europe. The French, for instance, before the Revolution read about the Milan tax in a detailed *Progress Report* published by Pompeo Neri for the Hapsburg leaders in 1750, or in the writings of François Véron de Forbonnois and Moreau de Beaumont; afterward studied it as the masters of North Italy; and finally drew inspiration from it in constructing their own cadaster under Napoleon.(8) Nor is it necessary to dwell on direct influences to give the Censimento a place in the history of France. Heated discussions among French officials, economists and interested parties about the manner of making assessments and deductions, the kind of personnel suitable for such work, the fiscal status of peasant laborers and sharecroppers, the problem of scattered holdings, and the crucial distinction between measuring single properties or only whole communities in block — all these had close or exact parallels in the long controversy over the Lombard reform.(9) With good reason the International Committee of Historical Sciences, in the 1920s and 30s, identified the land measurement scheme as perhaps the most characteristic undertaking of enlightened absolutism.(10)

Another reason for examining the Censimento anew is to test a standard over-all interpretation which no longer fully satisfies. Scholars, fascinated by the dramatic and intense conflict accompanying the reform at every step, have emphasized negative reactions and dismissed indigenous support as insignificant. The influential historian Franco Valsecchi treats the struggle as "a central episode in the battle between aristocracy and absolutism," and the crown as completely isolated.(11) In this view royal officials are so detached from Lombard society that the whole movement begun by the Censimento slowly loses its historic context, becoming, more than anything else, the unwilling agent of future times. Reformers, though not quite conscious of it, served the interests of an incipient bourgeoisie, and Milanese patricians like Pietro Verri and Cesare Beccaria, who helped to administer the land tax after 1760, were no less foreign to their environment than the leaders of the survey before its enactment, the Neapolitan Vincenzo Miro and the Tuscan Pompeo Neri.(12)

> In 18th century Lombardy there existed more a bourgeois spirit than a true and proper bourgeoisie ... The cause of the bourgeoisie was represented by an intellectual vanguard, by that new aristocracy which came to be called "bourgeois," the aristocracy of a Verri or a Beccaria, which fought for the economic, political and moral aspirations of a bourgeoisie in no position to act for itself.

In fact the extravagant conclusion quoted above does not follow necessarily from the arguments preceding it, and the author, Valsecchi, to whom it does little justice, himself supplies material for telling the story differently. Those behind the Censimento wished to benefit real groups in the land and expected, in return, that the inhabitants would reward them with aid and simpathy, which indeed were sometimes forthcoming. Feeling and speaking like outsiders when disappointed or aroused, they just as often labored to forge links between themselves and the public. One of their central achievements was the transformation of communal and provincial government, whereby a class of gentlemen proprietors, newly defined in the law, received considerable control over local affairs. Favor went to owners living in a noble style but feudal or civic titles hardly counted.(13) Here was an attempt to strengthen the monarchy while at the same time creating checks against it and allies for it. The combination, no doubt less coherent and convincing than programs of post-1789 democrats or liberals, deserves understanding in its own right. Labeling it bourgeois or magnifying the absolutist side are distortions which the present essay will avoid.

CHAPTER I

EARLY WORK ON THE TAX (1706-1733)

In the mid-18th century Austrian Lombardy, *lo stato di Milano,* was neither the most promising nor the least likely site of reform. With a population approaching one million, and an area of 4,250 square miles, it was sadly reduced from the great days of the Renaissance duchy. During the Spanish period various disasters afflicting the Mediterranean struck it hard, and in the forty years following 1706 Vienna gave away half its territory as the diplomatic price of keeping the rest.(14) Though nearly 200,000 people dwelt in six cities, commerce and manufacturing were decadent, a serious obstacle to general improvement. Agriculture on the other hand was fairly advanced, the universal activity in which farmers produced silk cocoons and cheese for distant markets, and escaped fallow by rotating wheat with corn, rice and pasture.(15) The social, political and administrative structure of Lombardy reflected imperfectly the devloution of the urban economy. Rural property was infeudated but less privileged than cities parasitically dominating the country-side. The elites, around one percent of the population, were above all landlords, owning four ninths of the usable surface and sharing in receipts from the two ninths belonging to the church. Yet they lived in cities, held key municipal posts and passed ordinances damaging to agriculture. They also fought amongst themselves, perhaps because in their monopoly of power below the level of the crown they had nothing to fear from the middle classes, the most active members of which were unpopular tax farmers and moneylenders, or dependent lessees of the big irrigated estates. At the top were the heads of Milan's three hundred patrician families, then came others of ''civil condition,'' about whom little is said or known, patricians from secondary provincial capitals and even towns, feudaries and some persons living nobly on the land itself.(16) Representing jurisdictions constantly squabbling over autonomy and privilege, they declaimed of equality and the need to redistribute burdens, and especially they attacked the preeminence of Milan. They may have found similarly disturbing the tension between city and country. Hence proper leadership might convince a few of them, and their constituents, that change was both urgent and desirable, while inducing others to cancel themselves out in mutual recrimination.

A week point in the uneasy equilibrium of the Lombard community was the system of direct taxation. It affected almost everyone and aggrieved many, objectively it was a major cause of desolation, and the Austrians, for fiscal reasons, were determined to make an issue of it. The largest single charge which Vienna inherited from Spanish rule was the *Mensuale,* a "monthly" tax falling on the provinces and capital cities in accordance with 16th century appraisals of agricultural and commercial worth. The honorable plan of Charles V and his governors had been to divide military costs with equity and regularity. However the land survey, completed in 1568, avoided mountainous regions considered too remote or exposed, and ignored some quite accessible properties on behalf of prominent owners; while neither records nor maps accompanied evaluations based on a partial sampling of sale deeds. The commercial assessment was never finished, and in 1599 arbitrary sums representing business activity were simply added to land values. Worse still, the Spaniards decided to use their information only for the establishment of provincial and metropolitan quotas, leaving further subdivision with local administrators rather than royal officials. The latter might have overcome institutional and technical faults, but the former manipulated them for their own interests and those of friends and patrons. No consistent measure told the individual of his responsibility, and burdens varied greatly from place to place. Everywhere the rural populace, small owners, tenants, sharecroppers, laborers and village tradesmen, "contributed" a personal tax which sometimes exceeded the real charge. The cities, on their side, upheld the traditional distinction between "rural" and "civil" land, whereby property belonging to someone living in (say) Milan, regardless of its actual location, was under the authority of the capital. Civil landlords benefited because an attendant increase in urban quotas did not fully match the value of their holdings, and because they could throw part of their expense onto the masses through higher consumption duties. They maintained and even enlarged this advantage in all subsequent disputs with the crown and the provinces, especially as *Mensuale* payments grew enormously during the wars of the 17th and early 18th centuries. Rural lands, usually the least productive of any region, were left with excessive taxes, touching off a scramble to change their status. Indeed since it was generally desirable to register property with local governments amenable to influence the movement from rural to civil was only

one of many "separations" occurring in the country-side to create a
mosaic of artifical jurisdictions. A sardonic passage in Neri's *Progress* •
Report suggests the total situation.

> Thus in a single community . . . there may be six types of property . . .
> with six different administrations . . . Civil lands are divided still
> further into the part of the harvest belonging to the landlord
> (*domenicale*), which is absolutely civil, and the peasant half, which I
> would call neither absolutely civil nor absolutely rural but an am-
> phibian which sometimes can be taxed by rural communities and
> sometimes not. I leave alone the more subtle question of whether the
> peasant half of civil lands is rural by its nature or by assignment and
> concession. If the latter, then it is divided into four parts, one rural and
> the others civil but collectable by rural people under certain con-
> ditions. In this case 100 *pertiche* of civil land would be divided into one
> part of 50 *pertiche,* another of 37½ and a final part of 12½ *pertiche.*

An important study ordered by the Censimento Commission in 1733
inspected eighty communes in ten provinces, comparing the incidence
of taxation in 1718 with new land evaluations. The experts discovered
that some communities paid ten percent of their capital values and
other owed less than one percent. Similar differences existed among
individual owners in the same commune.(17)

The Austrians, arriving in Milan in late 1706, first made the
Mensuale unbearable and then provided for its resolution. Governor
Eugene of Savoy changed its name to the *Diaria,* tightened its administration and raised its already high rates about ten percent,
demanding 22,000 *Lira* per day. Though impossible to collect in full,
the sum set residents as never before to ponder their financial plight.(18)
Systematic discussion began in 1709 when the mysterious Hapsburg
servant named Count Prass wrote a pamphlet claiming that better
methods of assessment and exaction must double the yield of the *Diaria*
while actually lightening its load on the people. Replies came from
oligarchic city agencies such as Milan's Council of Sixty, from
provincial syndics, officers of rural government probably no less urban
than the councilmen, and from the Congregation of State, a small
assembly of metropolitan and provincial delegates, likewise patrician
and noble, which since the 16th century had been involved in the
management of direct taxes.(19) These "public representatives,"
coopted or elected by narrow franchise, revealed little of popular
thought, but certainly they expressed the views of the potent men whom
Vienna had to convince and coerce before reform could take place. It is
therefore significant that the Prass controversy, if not actually encouraging, was ambivilent enough for the crown a few years later to
portray its redoing the work of Charles V as an answer to the "repreated

supplications'' of Lombardy for ''a new and universal evaluation and measurement.''(20)

Admittedly criticism of the *Progetto d'un nuovo sistema di taglia* was often rancorous and carping, and all rejected its primary aim of obtaining 15.5 million *lira* from the war tax. Milan and the province of Pavia even implied that Prass, the disciple of Marshal Vauban, was an unwitting tool of French subversion. Moreover the representatives asserted that the normal and binding means of gathering money for royal governments include many indirect and a few direct charges but excluded the major land taxes of Lombard history, the *Mensuale* and the *Diaria*, which instead were extraordinary subsidies or loans initially dependent upon the good will of subjects. Only specific agreements, the outcome of bargaining, would generate a moral obligation to support the costly European policies of Austria. On a more positive note it was said that legitimate taxes indeed should be equitable, and eloquent praise for a true measurement balanced the censure of Prass' crude scheme to assess wealth by counting acres and barely considering variations in land quality. ''Let no man believe,'' wrote provincial Pavia,

> that we approve ot unjust immunities or wish to profit from abuses. Too often this people has cried out for the removal of disorders . . . We have wished for justice in the past and do so for the future. The damage and wrong which overcharges the poor to compensate for exemptions given the powerful must cease.

However good arguments as well as bad can be used for selfish ends. Marcel Marion has explained how in 18th century France elites recommended ideal reforms precisely to forestall real action,(21) and in Lombardy some played the same game. Others were sincere in wanting a judicious survey because they assumed that the data would become the property of local officials and serve as a new prop for old practices.

Nonetheless debate over the *Progetto* was beneficial in that it made sectional rivalries more productive than usual. The overdrawn exposition of fiscal inequity and malfeasance drew from provincial and community representatives demands for redress, ''an apple of discord,'' as Milan bitterly called it, ''thrown among the publics to incite them to fight and destroy each other.'' Condemnation of Milan, even when particularist in origin, placed men in touch with concrete problems and breathed life into stagnating notions of equity and civic responsibility, which otherwise were employed with rhetorical flourish by all sides in any quarrel. With the privileged position of Milanese landowners a central feature of the current impasse, Cremona truly aided the crown by coupling a general plea for equal treatment with the accusation that the capital was paying less than half its proper annual assessment of 2.2

million *Lira.* Similarly Cremona's insistence that a new survey would take too long to complete and therefore was no solution for the *Diaria,* though unwise in precluding examination of a promising reform, indicated a genuine preference for results over words. Vigevano city proposed a measurement to sustain traditional prerogatives, and the town of Voghera advised that general surveys were impossible to accomplish with accuracy, but both were almost obsessive in requesting an equal distribution of direct taxes. Especially Vigevano showed that the universal dismissal of Prass was compatible with burning resentment against the advantages enjoyed by some native jurisdictions.

> Everyone realizes that each integral member of this domain was assigned its fair share of the *Mensuale* . . . Thus every city and every province . . . must carry in proportion all subsequent burdens including the *Diaria.*

It followed that the changes which many desired without knowing how to get them could not be trusted to those who previously had preyed on the weak. The provinces of Tortona and Pavia attacked Prass for expecting local governments to subdivide his immense quota, while provincial Vigevano groped toward the eventual mechanism of renewal by asking for a royal commission to referee the adjustment of rates.

Hence the opinion which Eugene's temporary ruling committee *(Giunta di Governo)* sent to Vienna in 1712, though neither summarizing nor presenting local views, remained faithful to the conditions and possibilities facing the dynasty in its new territory. Prass was unacceptable but the system of direct taxes should be overhauled anyway and the crown dominate the work.

> If, to obtain equality, it is necessary to evaluate the land in each part of every province, then we must be sure that the operation actually serves the cause of universal justice. Under imperial orders the existing measurement should be revised in general and through royal authority, as was done originally, not at the arbitrary will of the publics, from which could arise the absurdity of further inequities and benefits for the powerful.

The emperor agreed, and over the next few years his councilors decided upon an objective assessment of the land which would use Spanish precedents and rectify inequities caused by error, dishonesty and the passage of time. They hope to reduce the number and value of exemptions, not sweep away legal privileges or transform the society, and their agents on the spot would consider particular claims in good faith even while evolving a single plan for all Lombardy. For this limited task Vienna established in 1718 a royal commission or *Giunta,* and as a sign of strong support gave it equal status with the Milan Senate, the country's most respected institution. The Giunta members, five "foreigners" led by the Neapolitan Vincenzo Miro, had no hard and fast principles of fiscal order and only gradually learned what the Censimento might accomplish.(21a)

The internal record of the Miro Giunta, which held office from 1719 to 1733, when it was interrupted in mid-course by a Franco-Sardinian invasion associated with the War of Polish Succession, has been analyzed in fair detail by the historian Sergio Zaninelli, and only a brief description is required here. Zaninelli's main conclusion, already alluded to, is that the Giunta, far from beginning with the organic program suggested by Neri in a misleading passage of the *Progress Report,* proceeded empirically and almost haphazardly until the 1730s, at which time, in a series of brilliant memoranda, it brought together and articulated methods and ideas adopted along the way without particular sequence or unity.(22) The commissioners always spoke boldly but in the early years were unsure of themselves, especially because they knew little of the country. In April of 1719 they demanded information about land holdings from

every person of whatever state, grade, dignity, condition and eminence; however privileged or exempt by any mode, cause or title . . . whether foreign or native, absent or resident in any city, village, town, or place; possessing whatever property, lease, rent or income.

Then in 1724, and again in 1726, they carefully explained that claims of immunity needed checking precisely to avoid placing on tax rolls land which should be partly or completely exempt, for the violation of lawful privileges was "contrary to justice and to the mind of the Commission." Similarly the notification order of 1719 ignored the designation of property as rural or civil and forced owners to list their holdings with officials responsible for the jurisdiction in which the land was located; while the order of May 1721 announced that "separated" territories would be measured with their principal communes. Yet both proclamations depicted their ominous novelties as merely pragmatic actions intended to prevent "confusion, duplication and inconvenience" rather than make law. The second promised that unifications in progress would have no effect on the ultimate adjudication of appeals for separation. In 1727 Count Perlongo, an inspector dispatched from Vienna to see why the work was going so slowly, complained that the Giunta still lacked certain positions on matters like the separations and the status of rural and civil land. Indeed the members of the first Giunta never agreed about the church exemption, which was regulated only by the concordate of 1757, and their settlement for secular exemptions seemed expedient and arbitrary. In 1731 it was decided to accept the latter if they had clear titles based on honest transactions, but since most of them dated from the 15th and 16th centuries, they must be reduced to what they would have been worth against the relatively modest direct taxes existing in Lombardy in 1599. Later Neri censured his predecessors for being too lenient with charters of secular immunity and wanted to reopen the question of their legitimacy, creating machinery to examine them endlessly, using ever more rigorous standards and considering approvals provisional. Nonetheless he probably exaggerated when he said that the policies of Miro, including the failure to resolve the church question, had exempted half the land.(23) Seven years after he wrote the *Progress Report* the crown declared 85 percent of the land fully taxable, 64 million *scudi* out of a total capital value of 75 million, leaving a real exemption of 11 million *scudi.* Since the concordat exempted church property worth 9.5 million *scudi,* the laic benefit was perhaps 1.5 million, 2 percent of all land values. Neither this estimate, possibly too low, nor the figure of 4 percent found in a sample communal budget prepared in 1760 by Censimento leaders for agents in the field are large compared with the landed wealth of the Lombard nobility.(24)

Moreover the formula of 1731, insofar as it depended upon the ability of the Giunta to know how the old fiscal system operated, and to specify the situation of each piece of property, was a true innovation closely related to new principles of taxation.(24a) These all more or less stemmed from the fundamental point which Miro made in 1724 about the nature of his enterprise. The engineers, wishing to overcome various practical difficulties, asked him for permission to accomplish increasingly precise and detailed calculations of land value. Miro for his part was now disenchanted with the quality of information received from owners and concluded that his mission must be to establish primary evaluations instead of simply verifying statements of interested persons. Thus he was entirely agreeable when the engineers proposed actually to count mulberry plants on each property. There was an immediate outcry as Milan argued that the Censimento should only assign general quotas for use of provinces and capital cities. Miro, probably unaware of the full implications of his thought, replied that the reform was both general and particular (*particularissimo*), covering the whole country and yet fixing the tax of every individual owner. The renewal of Charles V's survey meant the correction, not the repetition, of abuses. This interpretation, quickly confirmed by Vienna, led first to a modern fiscal structure, and then to the transformation of all secondary levels of government, which in Lombardy customarily received and managed land tax quotas as a major function.

During the period 1730-33 the commissioners, now ready to employ their copious data, produced and perfected plans for a unified system of direct taxes that would merge numerous old charges — the *Diaria,* remnants of the *Mensuale* and the pre-Spanish salt and calvary taxes — into a lump sum imposed by the crown according to a single consistent administrative code. Though Miro died in 1731 his colleagues carried on splendidly, building the case for comprehensive reform out of a solid and profound knowledge of the country and the powerful planks of utility, regularity, reason and justice. They could prove that the familiar arrangement of two tiers which let local officials divide burdens among individuals, however essential so long as the cadaster supplied only general quotas, was the source of countless disorders, whereas through their labors since 1718 they had developed a different logic and ethic requiring the central government to control all assessments.(25)

> Our method follows necessarily from the fact that each property is described and evaluated in the new survey. If Tizio . . . is listed with so much capital value then . . . he must pay so much in taxes by the infallible rule of proportion. We cannot have public representatives do the figuring without nullifying the results of our work.

Secondly, by what might be called the law of coherence, once the crown could establish any part of a man's tax debt as a fraction of his capital value, it became mandatory to handle all direct taxes in the same way.

> The justice of such uniformity is self-evident. Since the state has been evaluated in geometric proportion among each possessor, any tax not so divided must be unjust, unequal and lacking in preceision.

Finally there was no further hesitation in solving the problem of territories and individuals separating from one another to reduce taxes. In private affairs men should not be forced into associations, but "honesty, equity and public utility were contravened when persons of any class who owed royal taxes . . . could escape payment with others of their jurisdiction on the pretence that an act of communion was never obligatory."(26) The designation of lands as civil or rural was simply another form of separation and quite intolerable despite titles and usage.

> These old manners, especially the distinction between civil and rural, often defended with the argument that one should not destroy venerable and supposedly fundamental rules, must be abolished without exception to satisfy reason and justice.

So the Giunta members, having demonstrated the "reason and utility" of their project, asked Vienna to end "all modes of tax distribution observed as abusive," and to charge secular owners, titled, distinguished or humble, solely at the site and by the measured value of property. Already they had entered the charmed circle of Enlightenment culture, imagining themselves on the threshold of ordering a traditional society which lived untidily among the landmarks of its history, one piled on the other.

The reformers consumed much time in gathering information and solving practical and logical problems in part because the work was intrinsically difficult, and even more because they were engaged in a constant struggle with indigenous notables whom they had to overcome or conciliate. Indeed determined opposition was largely responsible for the fact that Vienna did not resume the survey immediately after 1736 when the fighting ended in Lombardy, waiting instead until 1749 to appoint a second Giunta under Neri.(27) The politics of the Censimento were therefore always as important for Miro as technical developments and constitute an aspect of his tenure which must be discussed at some length. The standard view, to repeat, is that the crown, having few friends, mostly foreigners, and many enemies, was essentially alone. Certainly without Vienna, driven by the need of money, no new land tax would have emerged, as the Tuscan example suggests, for in the grand duchy an auspicious attempt to measure and evaluate farm holdings collapsed as soon as Peter Leopold and his advisers disagreed about the project and lost faith in it, though many subjects remained favorable.(28) In Lombardy the hostility of the Milanese patriciate, the one group experienced in planning national policies and transforming grievances into positive programs, allowed opponents easily to dominate debate outside the Giunta offices, while sympathetic residents were unorganized, timid and overly concerned with local interests. Nonetheless it is worth remembering that the latter might follow where they could not lead. The commissioners themselves stated that at crucial moments natives came to their aid with good effect, and this testimony, too often ignored by historians, deserves close examination. Even if exaggerated the reports reveal how royal agents expected and counted upon such assistance, drawing advantage and moral sustenance from perhaps just the shadow of it. Paying serious attention to the matter of support, in other words, offers valuable insight in the aims and purposes of the Censimento protagonists, who are not fully comprehensible when seen only in combat with unyielding forces.

The official stance of the government, a compound of wishful thinking, public relations and sincere belief, was that the evils of the Spanish tax made innovation acceptable to everybody, including those currently enjoying valuable privileges and exemptions. The claim that the Prass controversy had ended in a straightforward, general plea for something like the Censimento, a great simplification, entered quickly and glibly into the lore of reform.(29) In the *Progress Report* Neri wrote

that all kinds of families, "also the most noble," owned "rural" lands
on which they paid excessive duties, a curiosity explained by the
prevalence in Lombardy of profound ignorance about financial practices
and doctrines. "With the best intentions persons of every rank" feared
the new tax "against their own interests," of which they understood
little.(30) In truth a society so dependent upon agriculture desperately
needed laws that encouraged rather than undermined the country-side,
and on this basis the Austrian cadaster eventually was popular with the
upper classes, the Congregation of State agreeing in 1791 that it was the
finest in Europe.(31) When the Miro Giunta was formed, however, not
even the commissioners knew what to expect from their work, and the
overall operation of the fiscal system, as Neri indicated, was a mystery
to everyone, so that sensations of methodic injustice and demands for
wholesale change were quite lacking.(32) Perhaps too the study of
economics in Lombardy had not yet reached the point of establishing a
connection between fiscal order and the health of agriculture, though in
1710 provincial Pavia criticized Prass for not showing how his scheme
would provide for a rise in farm incomes sufficient to cover higher tax
rates.(33) Also in the first half of the century a severe depression gripped
the country, weighing against the prospect of economic improvement
through the adjustment of institutions.(34) While the first Giunta
lasted, until it had completed its investigations and formulated its
agruments, there was no widespread approval. Only during the period of
Neri's leadership could informed dissatisfaction with the present and
large hopes for the future, as inculcated by the reformers decade after
decade, become an essential background for the Censimento conflict and
begin to influence or determine positions taken by the various parties.

In any event Miro's strategy and tactics were not dependent upon the
theory of universal supplication. Since the opposition of some was
irreducible and related to solid interests, while others joined with the
government on particular issues for particular reasons, it seemed better
to meet the former head-on and occasionally rally the latter without
worrying about their general attitudes. Lombard nobles had learned to
live comfortably with economic stagnation and administrative confusion, but the privilege of actually flourishing from hard times was
distributed unevenly. Besides paying proportionately less in tribute the
Milanese patricians controlled the lucrative Bank of Santo Ambrogio
which supplied funds to communes bankrupted or impoverished by the
land tax; and the same system channelled an important part of the
country's wealth into the hands of petty rural politicians and
moneylenders.(35) The *Progress Report* which is usually cited as

evidence for the steady ferocity of the "census war" contains many references, in documents and commentary, to dissensions among elites and the rewards gained from manipulating them. If the author repeatedly attacked the Congregation of State, the national organ of the nobility, he also informed his readers that its considerable powers were wielded by an inner circle suspiciously eager to favor Milan. Thus he published a letter of 1724 in which Miro angrily charged the Congregation with bad faith, "and all the members composing it," then added the qualification, "to be more accurate, some members, especially from this city (Milan)," are at fault.(36) Moreover the Congregation was not Neri's only target, for he often spoke of the "secret enemies" of reform, an appelation hardly applying to the public activities of the representatives. His dramatic language, as well as alluding discretely to the powerful Milanese magnates, recalled the many bad and obscure local officials whom he denounced with force and detail almost from the first page of the book. Against these people — "a class of administrators who . . . nourish themselves on illicit profits" — he hoped that noblemen no less than the crown would be on guard.(37)

Political difficulties beset Miro from the start. In 1719 the Council General of Milan formed a special committee, the *Giunta Urbana,* to keep watch on the Censimento , and simultaneously the capital, whose chief civic officer, the Vicario of Provision, was president of the Congregation of State, organized a protest over the decision to use a technique of measurement unfamiliar to Lombardy. The dispute, lasting until 1720, raised some legitimate questions, but the royal commissioners, and later Neri, saw only procrastination and roughly imposed their plan, surveying the entire country in three years (1721-23).(38) However the fight had just begun since it was still necessary to evaluate property, an undertaking which commonly divided men and threatened the success or even completion of land tax reforms. In France during the Seven Years' War enemies of the *vingtième* always argued, more or less honestly, that servants of the central government were neither able nor willing to determine exactly how much the land could pay. The Physiocrats answered with a careful definition of net profit, though in 1763 Turgot admitted that a "science of estimation" was some years away.(39) The Tuscan effort mentioned above failed when the grand duke became convinced that appraising land accurately and in a way encouraging to agriculture was indeed impossible. Conversely papal leaders responsible for a survey in the territory of Bologna between 1789 and 1791 were all too sure of their competence in devising a tax. They estimated the net profit a property would produce if cultivated with maximum efficiency and expected owners receiving high assessments to obtain the needed money by making recommended improvements. Many complaints arose against the scheme, which the papacy shelved for various causes, and apparently the evaluations were impractical because in 1797 the French, applying them to a land tax, reduced them by half to bring them into line with the rest of the Cisalpine Republic.(40)

In Lombardy the Giunta members were both vigorous and cautious, defending their unpopular practice of making assessments themselves and receiving owner testimony as supplemental, yet wanting to please and help the landed classes. At first the problem was whether to base values on present productivity, the choice of Cremona, Novara and Vigevano, provinces with good but underworked soil, or on the raw potential of a farm, assuming no fixed investment, a course supported by the highly developed regions of Milan, Novara and Como. The Giunta, which feared that the second method involved too much speculation and would place a heavy burden on poorly cultivated lands, inducing their further deterioration, approved and enforced the first. Hence assessors took property as it was, noted the harvest, deducted standard growing costs, and computed market returns, the net and taxable income, with three sets of prices to adjust for the quality of terrain. Then they multiplied the year's profit by twenty-five to get the capital value, which figure they placed on the tax roll. Preliminary evaluations announced in 1726 evoked an immense clamor, and Vienna ordered revisions in 1728 and 1729. The Giunta was told that outside experts, appointed in conjunction with the Congregation of State, must join commission officials in reviewing complaints from public representatives as well as owners. The Congregation, already upset that crown surveyors were operating independently in the communes, had insisted that subjects could not judge the validity of their assessments without knowing about evaluations in all parts of the state. The representatives meeting together could fashion such a comprehensive picture and deserved a greater role in the work. A special brief from Milan and its territory repeated this contention in strident tones and demanded exemption for all improvements made since the 16th century. Miro, deeply annoyed at personal attacks against himself and his engineers, tried unsuccessfully to convince his superiors that the outcry was another form of delay, and he was shocked when Vienna, listening to his enemies, forced the Giunta to take strangers into its councils. The final evaluation of 1732, the one followed by Neri, was completed in a sour atmosphere.(41)

Miro's dread of contention and obstruction is understandable since lack of progress could become an excuse for giving up individual assessments in favor of municipal and provincial quotas, as Milan slily suggested in 1729, or for abandoning the measurement altogether, as happened after 1736.(42) Nevertheless the furor over evaluations also served the long term aims of reform. All along, Neri tells us, the commissioners sought to provide assessments that were "most mild, benign and advantageous for possessors."(43) To do this the engineers needed information about farming techniques, and consulting with owners and their representatives was as appropriate as interviewing peasants on the site. So long as the Giunta remained the authority of last resort the Congregation of State and the regional agencies were perfectly capable of assisting. In 1726 the Congregation, though determined that the survey would end in general quotas, made a sensible plea for distinguishing between the crude data collected by engineers and the polished conclusions expected from assessors.(44).

> Judgements of value, always difficult and complex, depend principally on knowing what a property can produce and what to deduct from the harvest for necessary costs.

Likewise the territory of Lodi sent to the Giunta in 1728 the detailed budget of an imaginary farm with an income of 2,617 *lira* and expenses totaling 2,332 *lira*. According to the covering letter:(45)

> The difficulty of evaluations is manifest unless one begins by inspecting the terrain in all communities, so remarkably different from one another, and the diligence of cultivation. The observer must realize that harvests sometimes are far larger than the soil could manage but for the expense and energy of the owner or impassioned laborer . . . Without close examination, therefore, we do not believe that it will be possible to maintain the equality desired in the Censimento.

Perhaps in response to such overtures, the majority of commissioners were more optimistic about dealing with the representatives than Miro, and early in 1727 they overruled him in deciding to give the Congregation of State the instructions which they had drawn up for their field engineers.(46)

The new college of engineers, six from the Giunta and six outsiders, convened in June of 1728 and sat almost continuously until 1732. Halting and anxious, these men settled countless appeals and re-evaluated most of the country satisfactorily for notables and the crown, a major accomplishment of the first Giunta. They focused on deductions as a matter of essential *(essenzialissimo)* importance, searching for expenses missed previously and granting precedence to advice from local representatives. Immediately they wrote off the part of the harvest kept

by sharecroppers and credited losses from bad weather and other natural
misfortunes; afterward they sanctioned and benefited two innovations of
Lombard agriculture more profitable and comforting to landlords than
peasants. One, the growing of rice, was increasingly popular with flat
land proprietors and lessees who wanted a crop suited to irrigated or
flooded fields, but roundly hated by laborers for the harsh and unsanitary conditions associated with it. The second novelty was a shift in
the dry hills from large sharecropping farms cultivated by extended
families or groups of families to units of less than five hectares where a
single small family, sharing and renting under a mixed contract, worked
the land with hoes and spades instead of the usual heavy plow. Through
this regime peasants planted market crops and turned the soil more
intensively without particular reward to themselves. The engineer's
summation of January 1732, written in the language of prudence and
compromise, clearly indicated how much had been conceded to owners
while obscuring the strong emotions of the period. Still it reflected an
overriding government committment that even the dead Miro could
have accepted.(47)

> We are certain that Divine Providence inspired His Majesty with this
> idea (the second revision) in order to assure proprietors once and for all
> that their assessments were fully justified. As our check of private
> correspondence was insufficient, we were commanded to compare
> every document with the comments of the provincial syndics. We
> returned to work acknowledging the need for more mature reflection
> and added new precautions to the ones we had taken before . . . In
> considering any province we would read the arguments of its rural and
> urban representatives, paying attention to the most minute point of
> the submission.

Indeed a century later the secretary of another censimento commission
in Lombardy, Carlo Lupi, looked back on the evaluations with near
delight. He thought that the Giunta members were no more impressed
with the initial assessment of 1724 than their critics and had published it
only to force owners to take them seriously and cooperate by giving
truthful information. Hence they willingly discussed the next
evaluations with the Congregation of State to aid provincial and communal officials and individual owners in finding errors and making
competent applications for relief. The Giunta, Lupi concluded, bowed
sympathetically before the Congregation's entreaty to verify the field
work of the engineers, "demonstrating its resolve to eliminate from the
minds of timid proprietors all suspicion and doubt."(48)

An especially tense episode within the evaluation process was the
counting of mulberry plants. Sericulture did well in Lombardy and the
Giunta reasonably wanted to include it in the tax base, though only by

charging mature plants of proven productivity. For most of 1724, until Vienna approved it, the plan encountered fierce opposition, inflamatory pamphlets claiming that it would take forever, send swarms of unreliable inspectors into the country-side and disturb everyone's livelihood. Milan asked the government to suspend the entire survey while this one aspect was discussed, a proposal which Miro saw as gravely threatening the Censimento because the court and public had little knowledge of such technical questions. Some of the trouble came from the fact that Milan's territory grew most of the mulberry plants and expected a heavy burden from the tax. However differences about the structure of politics and administration were equally important.(49) When the Giunta began measuring it was possible to believe that the results would be general and in need of refinement by the hierarchy of autonomous public corporations before distribution to individuals. Whereas the assignment of official values even to single plants awoke critics to the appearance of new information which regional and communal agents could not control in the traditional manner. An anonymous essay supporting the arguments of Milan stated again and again that the enumeration of mulberry plants was too specific to be consistent with the central requirement of any Lombard land survey, the establishment of fair quotas for provinces and capital cities.(50) Also coloring the dispute were vague hopes and fears that local governments robbed of their historic role in the fiscal system would themselves have to undergo transformation. Neither side fully articulated or anticipated this great reform but the logic of it hovered in the background. The author of the pro-Milan pamphlet wrote that the Censimento should improve the rules by which each city and province — ''the integral parts of the state'' — assented to its obligations. The survey was general precisely because it regulated the ''correspondence between publics,'' assessing proper rates for jurisdictions, ''so that they may be divided afterwards among owners.'' Neri discovered in the crisis of 1724 only the attempt to undermine the Giunta, ''and above all to halt its work at the level of provincial quotas, leaving further subdivision, as of old, in the hands of despotic public administrators.'' In the same vein Miro had said, ''those who govern the communes, and the mighty, wish to retain the arbrtrary power which they have so long enjoyed, being able to burden whom they please while exonerating themselves and their friends.''(51)

Yet this challenge to many profitable arrangements in Lombardy did not unite counselors of the upper classes against the crown. Indeed as Milan directed much of its annoyance at the other provinces for trying to overload producers of mulberry leaves, so the Giunta stressed every friendly move which the enumeration plan elicited in the Congregation of State. The commission report of October 1724 told Vienna that on August 14 the cities of Cremona, Tortona and Casal Maggiore tentatively accepted the counting of mulberry plants despite the objection of Milan. In later meetings and exchanges, after everyone had seen a full prospectus from the engineers, representatives from the first three areas, and others too, again gave their consent, nearly isolating the capital, which repeated its case and demanded that the favorable provinces deliver their opionins in writing. Impressed by such support the commissioners felt able to ignore Milan and make final preparations for the extraordinary survey.

> We pondered the evidence of the engineers . . . adducing the need for enumeration . . . We noted that many representatives insisted on the counting and others were indifferent or left the matter with us. The city and province of Vigevano flatly rejected the idea . . . and Milan was alone in offering (real) opposition.

At this point Miro wrote the heated letter to the governor, already quoted in another context, which first accused the entire Congregation of bad faith and then admitted that only some members, chiefly from Milan, were guilty.(52)

The combination of forces promoting resistance and cooperation in 1724 continued to influence the Censimento for many years. In particular attempts at supplementing the land tax with other duties reassembled the groups which faced each other on the enumeration issue. There was fair agreement that commercial activity should bear a light charge, the *mercimonio,* but bitter discord over taxing rural inhabitants.(53) The Giunta, though not enthusiastic, honored the Lombard custom that peasants, aside from their obligations as small owners, paid a personal tax intended to lower the sum which proprietors owed the state. Actually it is not clear what material interest anyone had in the *personale* since officials believed that owners rather than peasants normally carried it, directly or through loans and reduced rents, an administrative fiction which should be eliminated or made inconsequential. In 1757 the second Giunta wrote:(54)

> During early discussions of the tax public representatives raised many doubts about it . . . (The Giunta) replied that if the population consisted only of peasants (*coloni*) and landlords it would be a point of indifference to impose the tax or abolish it as the entire weight would always fall upon the latter. However other types of people lived in the country-side who did not depend on the proprietors and it would have been improper to free this group at the expense of the first two. Therefore the personal tax was retained and limited to seven *lira* per head, the industry of men without capital (*patrimonio*) being incapable of supporting a heavier burden . . . The other objection was that the personal tax should vary from province to province and commune to

commune . . . because agriculturalists in more fertile areas had larger incomes and ought to pay more. The Giunta, making every effort to reach the truth, discovered that there was no such inequality in the income of peasants as in every village contracts were regulated to leave them scarcely anything beyond food and clothing. The fertility or sterility of the soil was a question for owners and not peasants. When the land was fertile and worked at small expense the agriculturalists took a smaller portion of the harvest; and even when the content of their share was large, in a good year, they had so many extra expenses because of unsanitary work and other reasons that they were no richer than those living on sterile land.

Corroboration of this view comes from the modern agricultural historian Mario Romani, who calls the tax an integral part of farm labor costs; and from contemporary Tuscany, where in the 1770s large owners apparently let a peasant charge disappear on the understanding that rents would go up and that the government would facilitate annulment of contacts and leases protecting unwanted tenants.(55) Hence Lombard proprietors probably valued the *personale* more as an element of the status quo and a device for disciplining peasants, a hold over them, than as a fiscal relief.

In any event the Miro Giunta endorsed the personal tax only by stipulating its transformation into an institution of permanent uniformity, the same in every place and every year. The members wanted to end gross inequities existing within the tax itself, and even more to exclude all variance from the land tax, which could not operate throughout the country as a set percentage of capital values if owners divided more or less of it with rustics according to their residence or the location of their properties. After a long struggle the Giunta had its way, once again creating and using disputes inside the Congregation of State and between regions. The majority of provinces and cities, Milan leading, argued that the *personale* was not the commission's concern and should supplement the land tax solely as local councils saw fit, but Cremona and Novara, joined at times by Tortona, Casal Maggiore, Pavia and Lodi, affirmed that the two taxes were alike part of the Censimento and subject to general regulation. No doubt representatives of the latter jurisdictions preferred one rate for the personal tax, lowering the land tax of the whole state by a lump sum, because they thought that the densely populated Milan area would pay the most. On the other hand they must have realized from the debate which sounded about them that in siding with the Giunta on this issue they were giving vital assistance to the tax reform as a block and thus helping to liquidate the old polity.(56) The Milanese advocat Gabriele Verri, father of Pietro, declared that the controversy separated "a few cities hoping to profit from the populace of others to disburden themselves and the many publics which as lovers of justice . . . sustain that each community must decide for itself how to combine personal and real taxes.''(57) The commissioners were more explicit, insisting that the personal tax be included in the Censimento and not left to the arbitrary wishes of the publics. For tax purposes, they said, ''the state is one body and one province,'' and subjects everywhere must enjoy equal treatment, knowing what to pay the prince without depending on the strange calculations of their representatives.(58)

> There will be no more secrecy or abuse . . . and the science of taxation will cease being a mystery guarded by administrators.

Neri in his usual summary fashion added that the Giunta needed control of the *personale* to preserve the clarity which had been built into land assessments, otherwise ''communal representatives would have retained their ancient despotic powers, wilfully directing the real as well as the personal tax.''(59)

In September of 1724, before the enumeration fight was over, Miro asked the Congrgegation of State for advice on how he should handle the personal tax. His demand for immediate answers and the threat of unilateral government action stimulated divisions among the representatives. Cremona broke first, accepting a regular *personale* incorporated into the Censimento, and the turning point came in August of 1726 when the city of Novara took the same position in a comprehensive brief which supplied technical details and abstract arguments later adopted by the Giunta. The report of 1730 dwelt on the disunity and support which reformers had found in the Congregation and credited friendly representatives with advancing the cause.(60)

> The Giunta, desiring as much as is humanly possible to render perpetual the effects of this great work, shielding it from fraud and private passions, has adhered to the sentiments of those publics which request the uniform taxing of individuals in relief of the entire state . . . The city of Novara, in its presentation of 1725, amply demonstrated the necessity for a universal personal tax . . . responding most judiciously to the contrary arguments then in vogue . . . At that time Tortona agreed with Novara and does so today. The city of Cremona shared these sentiments from the first discussions . . . and still concurrs entirely with the Giunta. Casal Maggiore, with all its jurisdictions, follows the sentiments of Novara, Tortona and Cremona. The city of Pavia has made similar statements in the latest period.

Moreover, prompted by their experience with the personal tax, the Giunta members offered some general comments on the nature of opposition to the Censimento, warning Vienna never to assume that criticism signified any solid or unanimous opinion in Lombardy.

Specifically they attacked a petition just received in the imperial capital under the signatures of the Congregation of State and the city of Como.(61)

> But can there be any stronger reason for rejecting such complaints than the fact that this one has malevolently usurped the name of the Congregation without indicating to Your Majesty the extent of disagreement among publics composing it? . . . It is not possible to understand how anyone can send such a communcation . . . when at least half the cities of the state ask for the opposite.

So in 1732, despite lingering unrest, Vienna approved the Giunta proposal to impose on each rural male between 14 and 60 years a royal personal tax, an equal annual charge, which in aggregate would reduce the real tax in Lombardy by one fourth.(62)

The final serious encounter of the first Giunta began early in 1732 when the members announced their plan for a unified system of tax administration. After outlining a single method of imposition based on the detailed assessment of capital values, they defined Lombardy's crown obligation in direct taxes as the combined total of the *Diaria,* currently about five million *lira,* the special quartering expenses of 730,000 *lira* and the salt and cavalry taxes of 600,000 *lira.* The Congregation of State was mostly negative, denying that these duties, so diverse in origin and incidence, could be exacted indiscriminately from the whole state to burden people traditionally free of them. Conversely a minority of representatives from jurisdictions paying all or nearly all the taxes favored their distribution over the entire community. However this parochial display of selfishness was not the full story since as usual other, overriding issues were at stake, notably the imminent demise of agencies, interests and privileges connected with the old land tax, the associate civil, rural and "liberated" owners of Milan, Cremona and many lesser places.(63) The Congregation memorandum of May 1732 lamented that the new scheme would "alter and destroy the municipal laws, regulations, orders and usages of this dominion with regard to taxation," whereas the present arrangement, "giving the prince authority to impose tribute under law and subjects . . . the right of distributing and collecting it," maintained a division of functions "intrinsic to civil society."(64) The commissioners too were more engrossed in structural renewal than in the transfer of specific sums, promising rural owners help against the cities and individuals everywhere safety from the chicanery of local officials. An anonymous "Memorial for Use of the Giunta" stated that the reform, "introducing a perfect communion into the state," would solve the problem of unequal apportionment because "representatives from one province will be able to confront the powerful of other provinces more effectively.''(65) It is true that the attempts of the Giunta to gain allies was rewarded only by the clear support of Pavia city, but then consideration of the unified administration was hardly underway when the war put an end to all arguments. Indeed Neri described those in opposition as generally ''very honorable'' persons who simply misunderstood the situation and would have been horrified to discover that they were defending practices ''as contrary to public welfare as to their own interests.'' Meanwhile ''the few'' abhorring change for wicked reasons were constantly busy clouding the atmosphere and duping men of good faith.(66)

CHAPTER II

POMPEO NERI

Although the Miro Giunta did not finish its work, disbanding in circumstances of little honor or dignity, its achievement was immense. The Tuscan Neri, drawing upon the records of his predecessors, became sufficiently conversant with the fiscal problems of Lombardy to write the brilliant *Progress Report* in less than a year after arriving in 1749. He and his colleagues avoided the delays of exploring new ground and presented a decisive front to the opposition which was still very much alive in the country. With initial backing from the governor, Gianluca Pallavicini, the Genoise nobleman who obtained his appointment in the first place, Neri practically completed the Censimento in just nine years, including the reorganization of local administration, which was no part of Miro's legacy. Admittedly the second Giunta, like the first, fell from grace at the last minute, dismissed early in 1758 when another, less generous governor lost patience with it, and a cabal of Milanese patricians gained temporary influence in Vienna. But with such momentum nothing could stop the cadaster and two years later it passed smoothly enough into legislation. This success in the 1750s owed to Miro, to the generally consistent support of Maria Theresa's government, which needed money more than ever following the Succession War, to the talents and personality of Neri, and, despite contrary pressures, to an improved climate of opinion in Lombardy. A full narrative of the decade is difficult to construct because the *Progress Report* had no contemporary sequel except the scanty "Relazione del Censimento" which Gianrinaldo Carli, a later president of the tax, composed in the 1760s or 70s, and because archival materials are yet unsorted and unpusblished. However Miro's contribution already has been discussed, the role of Vienna is fairly obvious, something can be said of Neri and his reception, and, best of all, the reform speaks so eloquently for itself that a careful description of it reveals much about its historic setting and meaning.

Pompeo Neri was born in Florence in 1706, the son of an upper class professional family. Already in the mid-17th century the Neris were privileged citizens of Volterra, and the grandfather, Giovanni Iacopo, was physician to Ferdinando de Medici, the fragile heir of Cosimo III who later became Pompeo's godfather. His father, Giovanni Bonaventura, counselor for the grand ducal regime, was a distinguished professor of law at the University of Pisa, and his mother belonged to the Sienese patriciate. The boy studied both at Siena and Pisa, attaining the new chair of public law at his father's university when he was only twenty-one years old. For family reasons he soon moved back to Florence where he taught at the Studio Fiorentino until Gian Gastone, the last Medici ruler, made him auditor of the royal domain, which began his lifelong career in public administration. This post recommended Neri to the Hapsburg-Lorraine dynasty which upon assuming power in 1737 naturally was interested in the vast and complex Medici holdings. The newcomers, liking his ability and suggestions for reform, placed him in 1739 on the staff of the ruling committee as secretary for the finance council, and in 1745 gave him the astonishing commission of writing a modern law code for the country. But the last project, too ambitious for a barely established government, compromised Neri, whose rapid rise had caused jealousy among senior officials. Consequently Pallavicini's invitation to come to Milan and revive the land tax scheme probably pleased him as much as it did his rivals. In 1758 he returned to Florence one of the most accomplished and successful administrators of Italy, his reputation undamaged by the collapse of the second Giunta, and the highest state offices opened for him. The regency ennobled him and named him Councilor of Finance, while Peter Leopold, who reigned after 1765, took his advice on all matters, so for a few years he was a central figure in the famous Tuscan reform movement. In 1770, his paramountcy gone, he was President of the Council of State, and remained a respected elder statesman to his death in 1776.(67)

The dominant themes of Neri's public life were the law and state administration. Legal conceptions were dear to him, and he once interrupted a dissertation on the price of money to observe that the peaceful art of keeping men together in society rested on the fragmentary Roman codes.(68) More important, he made the law, rightly understood, an engine of government, the great tool of absolutism, writing in the *Progress Report*:(69)

> It is necessary to distinguish legislative commissions from those which are merely judicial. The judge must restrain himself within the limits of law and usage ... but the legislator, or someone responsible for

> proposing to the sovereign laws like the Censimento, can not and must not accept the encumbrance of existing laws and customs, even when these are perfectly legitimate in origin . . . New law introduces new right based solely on the interests of the state . . . Laws so justified need not give way before old regulatons which are superfluous or are to be reformed or nullified.

Hence this grand functionary of Hapsburg centralization, who knew as few others how to use legislation and the weight of government in dismantling and building institutions, consciously thought of law as creating no less than restricting power. His celebration of the state, while fully consistent with Italian jurisprudence, was also an end in itself, and he could argue that the dynastic ruler, representative of the common good, was right to drive through any kind of opposition. At the end of the *Progress Report* he resumed the assertion that Giunta decrees were legislative and not judicial.(70)

> In legal disputes private individuals may do all they can to defend their interests. On the contrary when the prince wishes to make a new law, though out of clemency he will explore in advance the sentiments of his subjects, the latter must content themselves with being heard and then submit quietly to the project which ministers deputed by the crown consider advantageous for the public . . . In no other way is it possible to make a new law.

Indeed Neri devoted himself to the consolidation of state sovereignty and royal authority, opposing every privilege or separation that claimed an independent source of legitimacy such as prescription. His aim in both Tuscany and Lombardy was a single society under a single political structure, and his chosen instrument of reform was the central government, *lo stato in corpo,* the associatim of the whole, which alone regarded general problems. One of his first significant tasks for the Hapsburgs in Florence was to enforce a ruling against the bearing of arms by church officials who believed that their daily activities were usually beyond the will of the prince. In the 1740s he adjusted the laws on entail *(fidecommesso)* and the seigniory, limiting the immunity of noble families from the crown and from time itself. Between 1759 and 1765, the outset of his second period in Tuscany, he led the regency fight against ecclesiastical mortmain and prepared arguments for abrogating church asylum and closing cloistral prisons. When Peter Leopold came to the throne it was Neri's proposal to create a firm basis for reform by first reducing the multiplicity of laws and jurisdictions in the country which won him the grand duke's confidence. In 1771 he was still engaged in this work as president of the commission giving Tuscany a uniform judicial administration, the fit end of his career.(71)

Yet Neri's absolute state was as much rehetoric and bluff as reality. In his political thought, perhaps tempered by recollections of the Florentine Republic and ideas concerning the freedom and welfare of proprietors, the legitimate prince, unlike the despot, not only respected his own laws but also reserved a formal place in government for elite groups and local councils. In 1748 he composed a long essay on the Tuscan nobility, background for the future law code, and without recommending any concrete action he illustrated the proper use of elites in the administration of a civilized society.(72) He began with natural nobility *(nobilità gentilizia)*, the distinction which public opinion spontaneously awarded families with many famous ancestors. While the rank sounded harmless, requiring neither office nor powers, Neri's description of it was curiously resentful. Men of natural nobility, he said, had their eyes uniquely on the past and their worst habit, the cause of much harm, was to discriminate against new nobles created by the sovereign for state service. Anyway the paper was mainly about civil nobility *(nobilità civile)*, the regulated association of subjects possessing special rights and duties of leadership. To obtain and hold the second title, which might be transmitted through inheritance, just the sanction of law, the ruler's consent, was needed, and within a given level of civil nobility all were equal regardless of family name or social prestige. These citizens, monopolizing government offices in a prescribed manner, formed the essential and inevitable aristocracy of communities based on consent, democracies as well as monarchies, and their privileges disappeared only when despotism or conquest effaced the social contract and deprived inhabitants of every protection. Neri was far from believing that the majority of men should have the "rights of government," and civil nobility emerged from the essay as perhaps the most effective and constant mechanism of inequality every devised, for the author stated again and again that differences between grades of statutory elites were slight compared with the supreme antithesis of citizen and non-citizen. A fascinating section on the history of Florence demonstrated both the heroism and exclusiveness of the first civil nobility to arise there since the barbarian invasions, the Popular Party which after 1250 saved the city's liberty and alone stood for the common good. Despite its name, guild organization and ostentatious hostility toward certain magnates, the party included "most of the old nobility, though not those notoriously Ghibeline and unfriendly to popular institutions, and the wealthiest families of middle extraction," to whom "was transferred the Civil Nobility of Florence," while "the little people played a part only through their obedience." Not that Neri bestowed unqualified praise on the Florentine civil nobility, which soon abused its power and drove the masses to revolt, making opposition of citizens and non-citizens the prime cause of instability in the city. He was too convinced that society had found in monarchy its "tutor, father and prince" ever to trust a republican aristocracy with sovereignty. Even so the Medici regime which followed was no solution for the problems of Florence, and this was the real lesson for Hapsburg ministers. The grand dukes naturally wanted to hold down the civil nobles whom they had supplanted but their methods were disastrous because the maintenance of positions without functions and the promiscuous recruitment of administrators from the people rendered state service meaningless.(73)

> So great has been the change over time in our mode of thinking about and evaluating the honors of citizenship that . . . office in the Supreme Magistracy, the traditional font of civil nobility, is now dispensed almost as a matter of princely clemency to miserable and abject men . . . The citizenry, enrolling the lowest plebians, was contemptible in the eyes of rich and noble countrymen and foreigners, and still today it is the same.

One might well conclude, though Neri did not say so, that the Medici had become despots.

In Lombardy, as we shall see, Neri tried to establish a medium rank civil nobility which could transform moribund or dishonest local governments into agencies responsive to the interests of the crown and large proprietors, vivifying the Censimento without being able to manipulate its clear and detailed regulations. His work of the 1750s attests this policy, though publicly he never articulated it except for a few hints in the *Progress Report,* and so does his conduct in Tuscany during the next decade when he and others founded the noted communal reforms of Peter Leopold. In 1763, as the regency drew to a close, he wrote two memoranda claiming that the Florentine Magistracy, an ubiquitous authority in the country, served the capital poorly and ruined the provinces. Repeating themes from fifteen years before, he explained that the Medici had undermined the power of republican offices and filled them with individuals who were "ignorant, poor and of low birth," whence the need for renovation. His essay of 1767 on the grain trade pointed out that the preponderance of Florence no longer had an economic basis since manufacturing and commerce were stagnant and agriculture was the country's major activity. Also in 1767, or perhaps in 1769, he sketched a draft program of provincial government. Three archaic councils, the Captains of the Guelph Party, the Nine Custodians and the Officials of the Rivers, which between them managed daily affairs almost everywhere, would merge into one supervisory bureau of modest importance. At present the members, drawn exclusively from the capital, decided all questions from the center, though they knew nothing of rural life, and allowed their local agents, the chancellors, to tyrannize the communes. Meanwhile in fragmented country jurisdictions representation was in the hands of peasants who abetted the chancellor's malpractice and obscured the voice of the richest taxpayers. This system, Neri argued, was inefficient and corrupt, and besides it defeated the rule that those who supported the state financially deserved a say in the expenditure of public funds. He counselled enlarging rural jurisdictions, restricting communal representation to taxpayers, and among them "persons with the most cultivation and credit," and placing in Florence a new chamber of provincial administration dominated by territorial members who would refrain from interfering too often in local business. Peter Leopold disagreed only on the issue of communal representation, thinking that regional government should not be limited to the rich and mighty, "who will oppress the others." Nonetheless the many assemblies set up in the 1770s, even if containing peasants, became instruments of landlord opinion just as the old adviser had wished.(74)

It is likely that Neri's economic understanding also inhibited him, despite his royalist posture, from invoking the full power of the prince. His outlook, practical and empirical as always, had an intellectual foundation in the brilliant writings of Sallustio Bandini, the first Tuscan of the century proposing organic renewal guided by economic considerations. Indeed Bandini deserves mention in his own right for anticipating features of the Censimento, while his life and thought indirectly suggest important forces at work in Lombardy and Tuscany during the reform era. His masterpiece, the *Discorso sopra la Maremma di Siena,* composed around 1737 and published in 1775, attacked the traditional metropolitan structure by which a few cities, especially Florence, regulated and harassed the land to keep food cheap and plentiful within the walls. Bandini wanted greater freedom for owners of farm products to seek the best markets and for rural communes to administer their own affairs; he also imagined a new land tax that would cut exemptions and introduce objective standards of assessment. Such changes, he promised, would pull the Maremma from its languor, stimulate general prosperity and increase crown revenue. Through the *Discourse,* so inadequately summarized here, Bandini passed on to the next generation, Neri's generation, the vision of an active landlord and agronomist protesting against the provision policy of all cities, and of a Sienese patrician venting ancient resentments against Florence. Perhaps too he refracted and made palatable for Italian state servants the explosive ideas of Boisguillebert, whose essays he had read and absorbed before 1737, and whose defense of agriculture and the countryside included mourning for the Estates General, an apology of the Fronde and sorrow at the decline of parliamentary remonstrance.(75) Thus the concerns of society, usually as perceived by noblemen, drifted upward to influence a design like the Censimento which monarchy presumed it was handing down from the top.

Neri probably met Bandini when he was a student in Siena from 1715 to 1722, and later may have helped him bring his views before the government and present his manuscript to the Hapsburg grand duke Francis Stephan. He was never simply a disciple, and details about the relationship of the two men are lacking, but his admiration was warm enough since in 1759 he persuaded the regency to house Bandini's vast book collection as a library for the people of Siena, and in 1775 participated in the decision to print the *Discourse* at public expense.(76) Moreover in the 1730s Neri was one of several officials urging from the inside what Bandini advocated from the outside, the release of Maremma grain for export, and after his Lombard sojourn he became the champion of this panacea. The famines of 1763 and 1766-67 gave him an opportunity to act decisively in the matter of grain regulation. In 1764 he communicated with Vienna behind the backs of his superiors and obtained a temporary concession of easy export. New restraints followed, and then terrible harvests, which finally drove the country, now ruled by Peter Leopold, to a radical solution. With the help of the sovereign Neri staged a series of ministerial debates that rallied liberal opinion and sanctioned a renewal of the 1764 decree. In 1767 the grand duke put him in charge of a special study commission, and on its recommendation enacted for all Tuscany a permanent system of internal and external free trade. The legislation, though marred by exceptions not removed until the 1780s, was famous in Europe and a milestone of the reign.(77)

At the height of the grain controversy, in 1767, Neri wrote two unpublished essays exemplifying his mature conception of political economy, which now rested on great administrative experience and wide reading as well as memories of Bandini. His ideas, those of a calm man who underwent no dramatic reversals or revelations, could not have been much different when he was in Lombardy.(78) One paper, a brief for government policy entitled *Sopra la materia frumentaria*, enjoyed royal patronage and circulated widely in Tuscany; the other was a memorandum on mendicity. Like Bandini Neri argued that governments wishing to benefit men, rich and poor, should let them pursue their private affairs rather than interfere in their lives. Also like the Sienese reformer he insisted that in Tuscany agriculture was the main source of wealth as the cities had lost the capital reserves and inventiveness needed to compete with transalpine business centers and rival local farm production: hence the crown should not block grain exports for the purpose of cheapening urban existence, nor generally favor municipalities over the country-side. However in discussing economic growth he parted company from Bandini by emphasizing the active role of landlords, whereas the latter, despite his aristocratic background and connections, had pictured them as consumers and even parasites while solititing friendly treatment for the peasantry with remarkable consistency. Neri offerd as the single counter to poverty and stagnation the prosperity of owners who employed city and rural workers, for public programs of construction, charity and provision were ineffectual or destructive. He knew that peasant farmers, no less than noblemen, used extra labor, but in the grain essay he noted how the small owners of Tuscany seldom lived beyond subsistence, and when writing about begging he defined the very word proprietor to mean someone with surplus funds. In this second opinion he specifically rejected, as Bandini had not, penalties for landlords too opulent to relish production, assuming that their preference for consumption instead of investment reflected bad laws and not just indulgence. He then gave a fine formulation of the 18th century thesis that material progress would ensue most rapidly after the revival and enrichment of the upper classes.

> Thus to impede mendicity one must increase popular subsistence, and to increase popular subsistence in a peaceful country which does not conquer there is no other way than to increase the riches of possessors and to give them the means to make greater expenditures. Conversely summoning owners to a new and more equal division of wealth is a project which has ever been a chimera. The riches of possessors can increase only by additions to agriculture, fishing and export manufacturing, the unique method whereby a land produces new nourishment and new wealth, and places owners in a position to increase their ranks and strength, recall the idle to labor and pay all workers hired for their comfort and luxury, and for their agricultural, fishing and mercantile undertakings.

The softening effect which Neri's cordiality toward landlords had on his absolutism is suggested by the fact that the references to peace and conquest followed from a rare criticism of Roman law for making the state excessively powerful. Roman leaders, he wrote in *Sopra la materia frumentaria,* opressed all those with a commercial interest in grain because they were soldiers who thought of provision as a military rather than an economic problem, passing laws which "in the situation of modern governments and monarchies would be ridiculous and infinitely prejudicial."(79)

Neri drew upon two apparently incompatible European movements, the authoritarian process of building continental states and the resurgence of aristocracy within the same heavy polities. He was an economic liberal who valued the power of government, and he supported representative institutions though certain that the prince possessed absolute sovereignty. In his time, place and social milieu, however, these tensions were mild and capable of constructive blending. Guardians of the fisc expected revenue from the affluence of subjects, and pioneers of laissez-faire needed a strong executive to dissolve old regime shackles on enterprise. Bandini reproached Florence, not the crown, and Neri distrusted men of title as patricians and feudaries, not as landlords and potential civil nobles. In the agrarian communities of Lombardy and Tuscany stable wealth and weak feudal organization made assessed landed income a measure of status and command which elites could accept, while the concern of royal servants for vital communal and provincial administration guaranteed that their aims were limited: neither side had to covet or fear the tax assembly as a weapon against monarchy. Franco Venturi says of Neri that he "carried with him to Milan the traditions and new ideas of a ruling class becoming reformist."(80) Indeed he was a "foreigner" who knew well the elevated world of his opponents, and the angry tones of the *Progress Report* did not exhaust his feelings about contemporary society, which overall were profoundly positive. If his work contributed in the 19th century to the formation of a very different civilization, industrial and bourgeois, this was unintentional.

CHAPTER III

COMPLETION OF THE TAX (1749-1758)

In Lombardy in the 1750s Neri finished the commercial and personal taxes; defended and consolidated the land survey and assessment; and created new machinery, political as well as administrative, to operate the system. The theory of the *mercimonio* was that it tax capital in traffic, not buildings or inventory, and exempt poor tradesmen whose income and possessions were insufficient to distinguish them sharply from wage laborers. The plan of 1732 had said no more on the matter of imposition, recommending only that the total bill derive from the average receipts of the period 1728-30. The second Giunta, perhaps finding arbitrary quotas distasteful, called for the interrogation of commercial people, by guild leaders in the towns and cities, by Censimento agents elsewhere, to determine yearly sales. Individuals would then pay 1¼ percent of their gross earnings. Actually it is doubtful that much detailed information was gathered and more likely that the crown decided in advance what it wanted from the tax. The annual intake of the *mercimonio* in the 1760s was approximately 138,000 *lira,* 117,000 from six cities and nine towns, and 21,000 from the 380 rural communes where noticeable mercantile activity existed. The cost for Milan was 60,000 *lira,* 33 percent less than under the old commercial tax. The cities and towns got their contributions through five year agreements with the guilds, which may or may not have bargained on the basis of 1¼ percent, and which dunned their own members almost as they pleased. Similarly communal officials seem to have relied less on declarations than on general estimates of how much rural business could and should pay. Once collected, the money was divided into two equal parts, half going to the crown in support of the land tax, and half remaining in the community for local use. The law of December 1755 which gave final form to the commercial tax, and the preliminary instructions of May 1754, while clearly exempting proprietors, sharecroppers, peasant lessees and salaried workers, left in confusion the status of small artisans — cobblers, masons and tailors without assistants or capital beyond their tools — and some of them eventually yielded up a few *lira*. On the other hand, after hesitating, the Giunta definitely decided to encourage agriculture by the exclusion of commercial leaseholders, ''who farm with the work of others and who profit from this labor and from the sale of produce.'' Indeed such men were often the best farmers in Lombardy, enriching themselves, the country and the great landlords. As for the personal tax, the main guidelines of 1732 were followed, the crown imposing a uniform burden on all rural and town males between 14 and 60 years, and subtracting the combined proceeds from the land tax to affect every owner equally. Neri having to specify the amount, rejected the idea that the *personale* should cut the real tax by one fourth, and instead established the figure of 3½ *lira* per person, which in 1760 brought in about 700,000 *lira*, 12 percent of the potential duty on land. It was also necessary to design a companion charge for the relief of local budgets, so the personal tax law of December 1755 required those responsible for it to pay a second sum, never exceeding 3½ *lira*, to the commune. The latter must decrease its share of the tax when debt repayments lowered expenses, and even assume a little of the royal portion if a suplus was obtained. By 1768 men in 250 villages and towns (out of nearly 1,500) paid less than 7 *lira*, and in a handful they paid less than 3½ *lira*. The commercial tax undoubtedly lacked the polish and precision of the rest of the Censimento, but its hasty resolution in 1755 removed it as a possible cause of delay, and it was never important enough to impair the working of other financial institutions. The personal tax was a disappointment in the sense that Neri and others hoped to abolish it altogether and shift its weight onto owners. Of itself, however, it was strong, simple and equitable, benefiting the peasantry slightly while fulfilling its primary task of protecting the land tax from indirect subversion.(81)

Anyway the description of the land and the principles of land taxation which the first Giunta had so carefully fashioned before 1733 constituted the heart of the reform. The new commissioners retrieved the maps and rolls, struck out territories lost from Hapsburg control and recorded changes in ownership, presenting Lombardy with an official survey of 810,000 hectares (2 million acres), three fourths of the entire surface, a wealth of information that quickly became a vital factor in the private regulation of agriculture, in the selling, leasing and renting of property, a special boon for owners who traditionally dominated the writing of contracts.(82) Neri also handled the assessment efficiently and with a balanced care for the state and the landed classes. The original evaluation, after deducting numerous expenses, calculated income by relating standard market prices to the productive quality of the soil. With wheat set at 10, 11, and 12 *lira* per *moggio* (3.3 bushels), and fields designated good, medium and poor, the worth of a "good" wheat field was the multiple of its normal net harvest and 12 *lira* per *moggio*.(83) In the 1750s apparently no one considered altering the assigned values to account for improvements in production or rising prices, though wheat was bringing on average 20 *lira* per *moggio*. Instead the country received assurance in 1760 that assessments were frozen into the foreseeable future, so the high prices of the next three decades, when wheat often topped 30 *lira* per *moggio,* and the growth in farm output, above all of mulberry leaves and silk cocoons, incurred no tax increases.(84) At the same time the total direct tax bill remained stationary, Vienna year after year imposing around 6 million *lira,* of which 12 percent came from the personal tax and 1 percent from the commercial tax. It is true that for a while owners had to pay fair sums to the communes and provinces — two sample budgets of 1760 indicate a local duty of about 13 pennies *(denari)* per *scudo* of capital value compared with 18 pennies for the royal tax — but in the long peace following 1763, as public debts were liquidated, this cost gradually diminished.(85) Already in 1767 the French economist François Véron de Forbonnois praised the Centimento for assessing land at less than half its true value, and a little later Gianrinaldo Carli, chief administrator of the tax between 1765 and 1780, boasted that it took from proprietors only 14 percent of their net agricultural income.(86) The 20th century historian C.A. Vianello hhas lowered Carli's estimate to 10 percent, the same figure found in a book by Vincenzo Dandolo, a fine Lombard agronomist and government official of the Napoleonic era, who in 1819 fondly recalled a wheat farm of the 1780s which on earnings of 15,800 *lira* per year gave 1,600 *lira* to the crown and almost nothing to the commune and province.(87)

Hence the land tax began with modest rates and the near permanence of its assessments was a constant spur to expansion. This "logic of the new census" provided the essential prerequisite for Dandolo's scheme of 1819 to animate farming in the dry hills by substituting vines and sericulture for wheat, a process which had long been under way spontaneously, and still in 1844 Carlo Cattaneo could exclaim: (88)

> What wisdom and fecundity in the principle as distinguished from those barbarous taxes . . . which are graduated according to yearly harvests and rents, a proportional fine on the activity of owners.

Neri wrote in the *Progress Report* that the Miro Giunta always intended to make evaluations "fixed" and "perpetual," but he gave no details on the decision and did not discuss its probable consequences for agriculture.(89) Carli, referring generally to the example of 17th century English fiscal practices, credited Neri in particular with convincing the government of Lombardy that it should facilitate production by not taxing improvements.(90) Certainly the latter idea was current among reformers in the early 1750s because in 1753 the Cremonese representative to the Congregation of State, Marchese Giambattista Freganeschi, explained how it would work in a pamphlet defending the Giunta. The province of Milan, the *Ducato,* had reopened the controversy over the enumeration of mulberry plants, complaining that counting them would leave the owner with a tax burden even after many of them died, a likely event given their frailty. Freganeschi, about whom more will be said later, composed a long reply in which he assumed without deep reflection that most men properly embraced the dictates of economic reason.(91) The popularity of mulberry plants in Lombardy showed that they were profitable beyond all costs, motive enough to raise them. The land tax simply would reinforce a natural bent as the government reminded subjects of their interests, compelling them to maintain the harvest and encouraging them to enlarge it. The error of critics was in thinking that after reform agriculture would stand still or falter.

> Such a conception is absolutely wrong since the census looks for fields to improve rather than deteriorate . . . We must believe that each person, in order to keep the profits of mulberry plants, will cultivate them diligently . . . If there has been so much attention to get this wealth before the enumeration, there will be at least as much, if not more, to conserve it, and also, if possible, to increase it, just because the plants are now taxed.

Moreover the material benefits accuring to individuals, welcome in themselves, would coincide with the justice of considering production a social duty for owners as well as workers.

> I am astonished how the (*Ducato*)syndics fail to realize that those who watch over their property should not be envied, and those who neglect their's deserve no pity . . . Men who might otherwise capriciously stop growing mulberry plants . . . are obliged to use their freedom well, an obligation so strict that anyone malicious and lazy in cultivating land . . . can rightly be punished, either in his person or through the forfeiture of idle fields, which should be assigned to someone capable of rendering them fruitful.

To tax non-existent plants was light discipline for irresponsible proprietors, seditious men defying their prince, ''noxious weeds which one extirpates from the ground.'' Though Freganeschi's argument ended in extravagance, his basic understanding of the Censimento, which offered landowners the prospect of private prosperity in return for a regulated and secure public income, was correct.

Admittedly the development of agriculture in the second half of the century was less substantial than its brilliant surface implied. The areal spread of traditional cultivation and the enrichment of old fields through labor management rarely involved major technical changes. Proprietors and publicists were so pleased with the situation on the land, calling it the best in Europe, that they consciously rejected the experiments of England, France and the Low Countries as unnecessary for Lombardy. Meanwhile the hill peasants who gave up wheat, mulberry leaves and silk cocoons in rents and debt payments lacked interest in raising commercial products well. Instead they concentrated almost fanatically on corn which exhausted the soil despite much turning and weeding and unbalanced their diet to make pellagra a serious health hazard.(92) However when the Giunta members made of the real tax a powerful economic measure they did not anticipate these bad side effects, and their intentions, which Carli articulated in 1768, are entirely noteworthy.(93)

> We give great encouragement to agriculture, a fact often missed by casual observers. This encouragement consists not only in the reliability of just institutions and the payment of an equal and proportionate share of the tribute, but also in the provision whereby improvements to the land . . . are exempted from all increase in taxation. Lands uncultivated at the time of the survey, and therefore valued at the minimum figure, even as they become cultivated and bountiful pay exactly the same tax as before. Conversely lands which previously were cultivated but through negligence or indifference are allowed to deteriorate obtain no relief from the first evaluation. With one stroke inertia is penalized and industry rewarded, solving a problem which has ever puzzled statesmen.

In consideration of such good wishes one may well ask whether during the 1750s the crown did not win the friendship of Lombard notables, especially since the reordering of local government, a matter discussed below, also favored the landlords. At first glance the answer is no, for many continued to oppose essential features of the Censimento like the enumeration of mulberry plants and the unified system of imposition. Moreover if Neri succeeded in keeping unwarranted secular immunities under five percent of capital values, on the other hand the exemption which the church received from the concordat of 1757 and the final settlement of individual assessment complaints entailed grievous defeats for him. He wanted for forgo half the taxes on ecclesiastical land acquired before 1550, whereas Governor Beltrame Cristiani, conceding 1575 as the normal year, gave full immunity to property worth 2.4 million *scudi*, and two thirds immunity to another 10.6 million, for a total exemption of 9.5 million *scudi*.(94) A more important issue separating the two men was the operation of the immunity, the means of taxing the fraction of pre-1575 land declared liable. The relevant sections of the concordat read as follows: (95)

> Article 3: The properties owned before the said date are indeed im-
> mune for the lord's portion *(porzione domenicale)* but not for the
> peasant's portion *(porzione colonica)*. The peasants on these immune
> lands must contribute to royal and local taxes on account of their
> portion at two thirds the rate which will be imposed for the same
> account upon peasants on laic lands. Article 6: The exaction will be
> made only on the peasants . . . and neither the church nor church
> owners *(padroni ecclesiastici)* may be distrubed on account of their
> portion.

This arrangement, truly frightening for Neri, threatened the fundamental claim of the census, that proprietors alone, no matter who
they were or where they lived, had responsibility for the real tax. Now
the government would abandon its clear conception and charge peasants
for land which they did not own and from which they drew insufficient
income to pay more than a token sum through the personal tax.(96) The
warning of the Giunta was stern and grave.(97)

> If we take the path of dividing the land into the lord's portion and the
> peasant's portion, and impose a tax for the latter on the actual person
> of the agriculturalist, we jeopardize implementation of the new sur-
> vey.

Unfortunately the commissioners were isolated, getting only vague
expressions of sympathy from the Congregation of State, while the
governor, busy negotiating with the papacy to lower tariffs at the mouth
of the Po, was openly annoyed at their abstruse arguments and
welcomed the concordat as a reasonable compromise which would
facilitate his commercial treaty and hasten on the Censimento. Worse
still the controversy convinced Cristiani that Neri was a cause of delay
rather than progress, and this belief, no doubt echoed by agents from
Milan, turned Vienna against the Tuscan. In March of 1758 the royal
ministers, with little insight or gratitude, dissolved the second Giunta
and placed in its stead a provisional commission made up of persons
close to the Milanese partrciate. The new officials, sitting until July of
1761, systematicially reduced assessments for wealthy owners of the
capital, an injustice which Neri never forgave, calling his successors
"vandals" in a letter of 1766.(98)

Yet it is a striking fact that in the end neither the concordat nor the
collapse of the Giunta were very damaging for the reform. The concordat called upon church peasants to pay their reduced *colonica* in the
same way as laic peasants, assuming or pretending that machinery for
collecting the tax already existed; but it did not exist and the government made no effort to create it. Without explanation or apology those
who later managed the land tax by-passed the peasants and charged the
church directly, which certainly was the simplest course of action. The

sample budget of 1760, issued by the provisional commission, listed the Benefice of N.N. in the owner's column, noted its capital value of 215 *scudi* and tax bill of 21 *lira*, deducted the immunity of 14 *lira*, and then put the remainder due, 7 *lira*, in the "has paid" column. The parsonage of s. Gio. in N.N. with a capital value of 91 *scudi* was immune except for a local tax of 2 pennies per *scudo* on the peasant's portion *(salvo per li Locali delle parte Colonica).* The five shilling charge appeared in the "has paid" column opposite the parsonage, which was in the owner's column.(99) A royal order of 1772 imposing 200,000 *lira* in taxes on the exempted church lands assigned one rate "for those churchmen who pay the peasant's portion" *(per quegli Ecclesiastici, che pagano la colonica),* and another, higher rate for the properties which in 1757 had obtained full immunity *(qu'pochi, che non pagano la colonica).*(100) So Neri's reversal amounted to awarding the church a larger exemption than he had planned, not the sacrifice of basic principles.(101) Similarly when enemies of the tax captured its controls in 1758 they satisfied themselves with adjusting evaluations and left alone the institutions, all of which gained force in 1760. Indeed the Censimento had strengths which not even Neri appreciated, and after 1749 its movement toward completion and relative perfection was ineluctable. For this the foreign champions deserve major credit, but the process is fully understandable only if seen as occuring within the bounds of indigenous opinion and desire. Whereas the opposition once easily dominated public debates, now local supporters of the crown spoke out with surprising cogency and conviction, a response to the *Progress Report* and the many pleas of the Giunta which must have heartened innovators and dismayed traditionalists.

Already in the 1740s representatives of Milan's *Ducato* began to use the language of weighty reform in a contest with the metropolis over troop quartering, the cost of which Miro had wanted included in the single tax. The provincials described the high aristocracy of the capital as too powerful for anyone's good and accused them of coercing and tricking weak rural communities into accepting inequitable and outrageous monetary burdens; then they raised far reaching questions about the fiscal system which so favored the city over the countryside.(102)

> To treat men equally, being equally subjects, the owners of rural land must never be taxed more than the owners of civil land, especially since the impost falls on the harvest, not on property as such, and fecundity does not increase or decrease just because land is described as rural or civil.

Nonetheless the authors employed these arguments only in defense of local interests and, far from making them general, easily ignored or contradicted them for similar purposes. Claiming a common responsibility with the city of Milan for certain taxes, they also denied any larger fellowship which might require them to share expenses and regulations with distant jurisdictions.(103) If the Milanese aristrocracy sometimes was oppressive, on the other hand a major and inalienable privilege allowed *Ducato* landowners to become members of the very same noble order.(104) In sum the point of the historian Valsecchi, that regional elites who enthusiastically attacked Milan were equally quick to resist innovations threatening themselves, applies extremely well to officials in the capital province.(105)

Beyond the circle of Milanese influence, however, particular grievances developed into solid doctrines and convictions for comprehensive renewal. In 1758 the *Ducato* criticized the idea of a unified financial administration, practically in existence, by rejecting all liability for the cavalry tax. The joint reply of Cremona, Lodi, Pavia and Casal Maggiore was a powerful vindication of the Censimento and its underlying principles.(106) The statement, signed by country as well as urban representatives, rural Casal Maggiore excepted, often met specific objections of the *Ducato* with stilted and old-fashioned rebutals, but as often it broke through the stale traditions of inter-provincial disputation to reach for a new concept of the state in which centralized government and increased royal power actually enriched the lives of subjects, both spiritually and materially. Customary practices were of no matter, the syndics and orators said, for if a prince had previously imposed taxes on one province and not another, nothing prevented his successors from using a ''far more praiseworthy discretion (*arbitrio*)'' to demand equal tribute from everyone. Indeed Maria Theresa had done just this when she appointed Neri, as a quotation in capital letters from the imperial dispatch of July 1749 demonstrated.

> We WISH as a FUNDAMENTAL MAXIM that an EXACT PROPORTION BETWEEN DUTIES and the subject's RESPECTIVE SUBSTANCE be observed in ALL ASSIGNMENTS made in the state.

Moreover these words, sufficient in themselves, corresponded with the cumulative actions of the commissioners, whose intentions were likewise unmistakable.

> The Giunta has declared in endless rulings, tacitly and explicitly, that the maxims of the census make common what was once private . . . and that individuals or communities formerly free not to pay must contribute now.

The advocates concluded with the impressive remark that the costs of the survey would be wasted until ''all sons of the supreme father and head of the republic, good brothers and associates,'' were brought to give in perfect proportion for the defense and conservation of the ''mystic body politic *(mistico sociale corpo)*.''

First to sign the joint reply, perhaps its author, was the leader of Cremona city, Giambattista Freganeschi, whose thoughts on the economic effect of the land tax were noted above. The overall attitude of this member of a distinguished Cremonese family — his father held the post of orator before him — is difficult to define, for he was a passionate controversialist and has been praised or criticized from the most diverse points of view. In the 1750s his enemies considered him a perverse defender of Giunta policies; in the 1760s Pietro Verri and the Lombard governor *(ministro plenipotenziario)*, Carlo Firmian, believed that he was part of a patrician conspiracy to undo the entire Hapsburg reform program; and in the 1890s an economist named C.A. Conigliani described him as the major liberal opponent of the Censimento. (107) The last interpretation rests on two essays written in 1759 and 1787, apparently by Freganeschi, which stated flatly that the new survey, even if an improvement over the old, was profoundly mistaken in conception and execution because it had evaluated potential rather than actual production, taken too long and cost too much, ended in an unworkable hodge-podge of instructions and regulations, and sealed itself off from future improvement by the pretense of perpetual validity. Instead the government should have equated value with the intensity of labor, charging owners, through a salt tax, according to the number of peasants working their lands. If these were Freganeschi's sentiments, they strangely conflicted with the joint reply, the treatise on mulberry enumeration and two other essays which he composed in the 1750s, none of them known to Conigliani.(108)

Two pamphlets published in 1752 and 1753 dealt with the continuing agitation over the personal tax. Freganeschi certainly wanted the fiscal system to take adequate account of population distribution, and perhaps, without saying so, he felt that the Censimento was not going far enough in this direction; but in general he evinced a high regard for the work of the Giunta members, including their attempt to found a new kind of polity in Lombardy. Like Miro and Neri he claimed that opposition to the survey, the cause of its long delay, was in bad faith, the strategem of private persons and even representatives more concerned with their own interests than those of the community. Besides the Giunta plan to encumber rural residents at a flat rate which the crown set and received was appropriate because populous provinces such as the *Ducato* thereby would pay a fairer share of direct taxes, and because individual communes were notoriously incapable, whether from malice or incompetence, of imposing the *personali* with equity and justice. Syndics for the Milanese duchy soon replied, declaring that Freganeschi had no allies in the Congregation of State and few adherents in Cremona itself. More important his uniform personal tax was repugnant in a state composed of provinces which never had formed and never should form an integrated socity. *The Ducato,* Cremona and the others, ''a loose collection of peoples,'' were associated only by their subjection to the same crown, which neither created obligations between them nor influenced their internal constitutions. Vienna could assign a total sum for the personal tax, a percentage of the land tax, but the secondary divisions, as well as the proceeds, must stay in the communities to insure that peasants made payments commensurate with their incomes, and that they relieved the burden of owners truly deserving their support. This brief of 6 March 1753 in turn provoked a ''Confutation'' from Freganeschi, who insisted that other representatives agreed with him, ,as did the citizens and General Council of Cremona city. His critics, for their part, had ''dared to offend the Royal Giunta, and with it truth and justice.'' On the substance of the matter, Lombardy was indeed a ''civil society,'' making the uniform personal tax entirely legitimate. The exchange concluded with a defense of the *Ducato* by the Milanese advocate Giovanni Montorfani. A civil society between two provinces, he said, supposed their union, a degree of mutuality which no one could derive from the mere fact that they had a common sovereign. Actually Milan was tied to Cremona only as much as to the Hapsburg lands in Flanders and Germany.(109)

> All the subjects (of the State of Milan) have a general duty to contribute to the prince, who protects the persons and property of all generally. However it must be understood that the generality (in duties) is locked within the confines of each separate province.

Meanwhile the two provinces were arguing about the enumeration of mulberry plants, the occasion for Freganeschi's third pro-government pamphlet, probably written in early 1753. Once again the orator used ideas found in the *Progress Report,* and he also anticipated the joint reply. In the first place objections based on prescription or the fundamental traditions of Lombard history were invalid, for the Giunta properly did what was required to fulfill its task of establishing equitable fiscal laws. ''Here is justice, here is utility, whence arises the necessity of accepting any novelty.'' Direct taxes were now undoubtedly common to every part of the state and so the crown should assign them all proportionately and individually, while a return to quotas would serve communities seeking escape from their responsibilities."To be general the Censimento precisely must be particular." Fraganeschi then analyzed the enumeration question in detail, affirming the new methods of evaluation with arguments which, almost point for point, depart from the position attributed to him by Conigliani. When valuing the mulberry plants, and all other crops, the assessors had rightly reported only current production, not the soil's potential, which never could be determined. The results were fair and operated in a way that made the survey useful for many years, though not forever, as no work of man was permanent.

> The principal object for those who impugn the enumeration as for those who promote it must be the introduction of proportions which are accurate and will remain so in a census meant to endure. To this provident purpose the scheme devised by the Giunta and executed by the engineers . . . contributes admirably.

Hence time and money were well spent on the reform, which anyway would have been completed long before and at modest cost had not interested parties blocked it in order to maintain their indecent privileges and advantages. The author ended with more compliments for the Giunta and the plea that in future discussions the *Ducato* syndics follow the dictates of patriotism and justice.(110)

Despite contradictions in Freganeschi's thought and the possibility that his commitment to the Censimento was temporary, the trenchany and elevation of his positive statements are impressive. Moreover in this posture he was not alone as the Milanese asserted. Outlying provinces, especially Cremona, wanted significant improvement in the tax structure at least since the announcement of the Prass plan in 1709. Miro received useful aid from their representatives at critical moments of the first Giunta and during Neri's tenure they upheld the government in general terms no longer vitiated by regional prejudice. The joint reply and the writings of Freganeschi spoke for local aspirations and energies ready to join with foreign administrators in constructing a more cohesive and modern community out of the weakly federated jurisdictions of old Lombardy. These efforts lacked the consistency and power of the resistance centered in Milan, for patricians of the capital, fearing great loss from the equal treatment of all provinces and from the curtailment of urban dominance, knew better how to influence agencies like the Congregation of State and lobby in Vienna, as the last minute lowering of their assessments and the fall of Neri indicated. Nonetheless any gesture of friendship from the upper classes was valuable for reformers who designed institutions and legislation to facilitate cooperation between monarchy and elites, an essential basis for the humane and productive society of their dreams. Indeed at the very time that Freganeschi was preparing his blasts against Milan the Giunta began a series of political changes in the communes, provinces and cities which aimed at cementing just such an alliance even while pushing the tax ahead and strengthening the authority of the ruler.

CHAPTER IV

THE REFORM OF LOCAL GOVERNMENT

The transformation of local and regional government after 1753 complemented the fiscal system by associating status and royal benefits with certain sorts of economic success rather than birth or title. As the crown insisted that lay proprietors pay the land tax regardless of rank, and expected them to profit from favorable sections of the law in accordance with their wealth and ability, so it reserved for them the secondary levels of administration because they owned taxable land, especially valuable and appreciating land. There was no thought of replacing the nobility with a different class or creating a markedly fluid society in which men moved easily from bottom or middle to the top. Instead the program invited existing elites to renew themselves without loss of gentility, to become more active and open to change, more deserving of their high place. Even the urban patricians who relinquished important privileges could maintain power by emphasizing the fact that they were landowners and direct or indirect servants of agriculture. Perhaps this kind of reform, a blend of old and new, was in the back of Neri's mind from the beginning, since his *Progress Report,* in dwelling on the poor management of communes as a central cause of tax inequity, established the need not only to purify the village councils but also to give them a different social foundation. Specifically the first task of reformers bringing the poor justice was the removal of middling and humble men from office. For Neri, no prophet of bourgeois ascendency, the villain and symbol of rural malaise was the *esattore,* a person who advanced money to the commune for taxes and collected his costs and profits from owners and workers at harvest time. Unfortunately the exactor, though well-off, was not a gentleman: an unscrupulous moneylender (*usuriere di campagna*), he wanted vast returns from his little pile (*piccolo peculio*) instead of the normal and proper ''mercantile interest.'' In addition he used his financial leverage to dominate the village council and often illegally assumed a key position himself. Hence everywhere small fry administrators (*spicciolati am-*

ministratori) exploited their influence for personal gain and allowed favorites to evade taxes. Leaders in the country-side were men of proven ability who lacked honor and blocked the way to progress.

> Anyone familiar with the class of individuals usually composing the communal councils knows that public administration must fall to two or three residents with money, talent and aptitude (*denaro, talento, aderenze*), whom the multitude place in charge . . . And if they are dishonest, as too frequently happens, the communal patrimony is in danger.

For these political ills the compound cure which Neri implied in 1749 and instituted during the next decade was to increase royal control over the communities and to provide them with the interest and intervention of private subjects who were "vigilant and affectionate toward the common good."(111)

Neri's analysis was logical enough. The communal officials, constantly having to defend their jurisdictions from powerful ecclesiastics and noblemen in search of tax benefits, were inadequate partly because of their lowly station. Even when honest they were unlikely disputants in the many law suits which patrician landlords drew to capital cities under their control. At home they hardly could avoid breaches of trust in administering obscure and contradictory laws, nor would geographic and social proximity necessarily make them solicitous for the weak and poor. Regulations forbidding the exactor to hold political office undoubtedly signified a long experience of collusion.(112) Yet sympathy for the peasantry was only one of several factors motivating Neri. As is clear from his Tuscan activities, he also believed that the lower classes were incapable of ruling themselves, and wished to prevent them from using their majority against legitimate interests of the wealthy. Indeed the opinion was common in Italy that plebians should stay outside of local government not so much to avoid corruption as to leave questions about property exclusively in the hands of substantial owners. In Lombardy itself some people soon decided that the Giunta president had not done enough in restricting institutions of popular representation, and even before 1760 they attempted to improve upon his work.(113) When the Censimento became operative in Mantua after 1786 landless pesants who traditionally participated in communal meetings with full rights suffered a definite loss of influence.(114) About the same time the open assemblies of rural Naples, which opposed the division of common lands and harassed commercial farmers by limiting the movement of grain during scarce years, came under increasing attack. In 1806 a comprehensive law barred from village councils all men without a specified landed income.(115)

However in Lombardy the hostility toward peasant councilors was only the negative side of a most impressive and positive programe deserving full elucidation. The Neri Giunta announced its intention to organize anew the country's almost 1,500 communes on April 7, 1753, stating that the imminent publication of modern tax rolls required the creation of a forum where assessed owners (*estimati*) could discuss affairs and safeguard their interests by the election of "legitimate" agents. The reformers also wanted improved procedures for representation so that tax evaders and malevolent opponents of the Censimento never again could pretend to speak for whole communities. Consequently the owners of a commune, or their substitutes, joined together in convocation and selected from their number two second rank deputies. The first deputy was automatically the person paying the most in real taxes. The three representatives then became the official channel of communication between the Giunta and the proprietors. For the moment they worked beside incumbent village leaders who continued in charge of matters not connected with the Censimento.(116)

In December of 1755 the crown issued permanent and sweeping regulations on rural government which superseded the ancient system entirely. The law of communal reform, covering fifty printed pages, was an eloquent recital of 18th century ideals and aspirations.(117)

> In each territory . . . must be formed a single convocation of tax paying owners, and from the convocation must be taken one deputation only, one representation, one government, one administration . . . reducing all proprietors to one society, subject to one impost, one evaluation, equal and indivisible.

> All territorial fragments, all divisions and subdivisions of communal administration, all corps, all colleges, all separations . . . are abolished . . . All and every distinction of ownership is abolished . . . Moreover we do command the express and absolute suppression of every distinction between rural and civil property and every subdivision of rural and civil owners . . . whereby all properties described in the communal maps and tables are of one nature alone, one qualification alone . . . Without considering former names or distinctions such properties are equally taxable and equally responsible to uphold and maintain in proportion to their worth the fundamental rights of the state . . . Her Majesty wishes to ensure for all future times the total equality of property.

At the core of this polity, implemented slowly over the next four years, was the convocation which admitted without regard for rank all adult males inscribed on the property tax rolls. Women and minors could vote by proxy, and the only owners systematically excluded were those enjoying or claiming exemptions on more than half their land values in the jurisdiction, so that the formal denomination for the principal participant, *estimato,* was a title of honor and dignity, contrasting sharply with the French notion of *taillable.* The property qualification, without downward limit, was in itself almost democratic. Roughly one in five Lombard inhabitants held land, and assemblies in all areas welcomed peasant owners, especially in the mountains, a region of small plots, though also in the hills and plains where over eighty percent of the proprietors had less than six hectares.(118)

> In the convocation every entrant will have a voice equal to any other no matter what his tax rate, and each will have one vote whatever the number of his properties.

On the other hand peasant *estimati,* except in the mountains, generally supplemented their incomes by sharecropping or laboring for large owners, to whom they were also in debt, a dependent situation which imparied their numerical strength.(119) Anyway a subordinate and deferential role for them in the community was precisely the aim of the Giunta, which carefully withheld powers from the personal tax deputy, the only official directly responsible to the rural masses. Whereas the law encouraged wealthy members of the convocation to dominate its affairs by insisting that absentee owners receive advance notice of all meetings and allowing them to appoint delegates if they could not attend in person. Similarly the property deputies, leaders of the assembly, could live in the cities and send substitutes, an important right since the first ranking deputy was chosen from the three richest owners of the jurisdiction and likely would be an urban resident.(120) Altogether the convocation was a remarkable institution, animating a traditional society with liberal and judicious local government even as it brought the country-side new disparity and friction. There is truth as well as illusion in the words of Carlo Cattaneo, who described the act of 1755 as a pure mixture of "providence, justice and, what will seem most strange, liberty." It was, he said, "the voice of a philosopher speaking to a people already free and deserving to be free."(121)

The convocation met twice a year to administer taxes and decide on local improvement projects or the hiring of teachers and doctors. In January the landowners distributed tax quotas in accordance with the Censimento tables and regulations, and in the fall they elected three "property" deputies *(deputati dell'estimo)* by secret ballot. The latter, though sharing some power with two other deputies, one each for the personal and commercial taxes, were the executives of the commune. They presided over the convocation, supervised all business when the assembly was not in session and alone represented the whole community before the Giunta and successive royal tax commissions. They also directed the exactor and the syndic *(sindaco)*, a salaried official residing in the commune who managed daily affairs for absentee or unavailable deputies. Such arrangements placed local administration firmly in the hands of property holders, especially substantial ones, making it less rustic than apparently it had been in the past. The convocation, itself based on propety, installed proprietors as deputies, and likewise proprietors as *revisori*, two members of the assembly named each year to check the financial records. The property deputies acted with ''due dependence on the convocation'' and knew that while absent their substitutes in turn were under steady obligation to consult with them. For good measure the Giunta warned them to appoint as substitutes ''persons of probity capable in need of serving the public interest.'' Provision for the syndic, who himself did not have to own land, equally favored proprietory rule, since after his election by all five members of the communal government he became an agent of the property deputies.(122)

> In contracts the syndic represents and commits the community, understanding however that in all things he must proceed with the counsel and approval, consent or instruction of the property deputies, upon whose ordination he relies.

The best example of the command chain imposed by Neri is the mandate which he granted the owners to control the exactor, once a power unto himself in the villages. Forty-three articles minutely described the work of this entrepreneur, specifying his rights and duties so that everyone could see when he was at fault. Moreover the act had communes combine by counties *(delegazioni)* for the purpose of overawing the exactor in discussions about his contract. In the final meeting only property deputies negotiated for the communes, and neither syndics nor personal and commercial deputies could attend.

> The property deputies of the several communes will come together in the county office and arrange a multiple contract that will give the best service at the least cost. By setting one large contract the deputies can obtain easy terms because the exactor chosen by an entire county will lack the advantages of personal ties and high regard which he might enjoy when dealing with the administrators of one community.

Preceding the negotiations was a public auction where the property deputies kept order and gave preference to the lowest bidder among those offering themselves for the position of exactor. A single commune could follow this system without the rest of its county, but deputies wanting simple contracts needed to satisfy the crown that they intended some clear benefit for their constituents and that there was no collusion between themselves and any prospective tax collector. The Giunta also threatened communal officials with a 6,000 *lira* fine and loss of place should they participate even indirectly in the profits of the exactor, who for his part could not be the family relation of an administrator.(123)

Admittedly the reformers tempered the power of landowners by establishing separate deputies for the personal and commercial taxes. Once a year, like the owners, individuals on the personal and commercial rolls met in distinct groups to elect one of their number as deputy: all resident males between 14 and 60 years for the *personale;* merchants and artisans with capital beyong hand tools and profits above subsistence level for the *mercimonio.* The men chosen could be proprietors but not absentee since in the latter status they would bear neither tax. The duties of the personal deputy, who represented most families under the commune's jurisdiction, were impressive enough. The tax, as we know, began at 7 *lira,* 3½ for the central government and up to 3½ for the locality depending on need. The deputy made sure that the commune never took more than 3½ *lira* and that it demanded even less from the peasantry as expenses fell. He also could resist owners attempting either to cut their contribution through the reduction of essential communal services or to spend too much on works of little value for the majority of inhabitants. Moreover a striking passage in the law told the personal deputy to watch over the common lands and raise the alarm whenever owners should consider selling, renting or in any way disposing of areas customarily available for "promiscuous enjoyment." Given the hostility of European political economists toward commons, this support for the Lombard peasants against their landlords is surprising and reflects well on Neri, who certainly wished for the technical improvement of agriculture. The personal deputy fulfilled his office by attending convocations of property holders and meetings of the landed deputies. On these occasions he spoke for the rural masses and if he was dissatisfied with the policies of his fellow officials he could appeal to the crown for help. The Giunta did not describe in detail the tasks of the commercial deputy, who came from a small constituency, but he had general authority to act as the personal deputy when his group felt endangered.(124)

Cattaneo, looking back from the 19th century, saw in the balancing role of the personal and commercial deputies a generous concession to universal sufferage; Pietro Verri probably had the same thing in mind when he praised Maria Theresa for introducing "democratic government" into the country-side; and Gianrinaldo Carlo, who knew the most, said flatly that local administration was the charge of all five deputies.(125) Such assessments, though indicating a notable feature of the communal reform law, exaggerate the force and leverage which the Neri Giunta turned over the plebian leaders. The landowners had their first convocations and deputies from the temporary act of April 1753, while personal and commercial tax payers received similar permission to convene and elect only in May of 1754 and lacked complete information about the prerogatives of their deputies until the appearance of general legislation in late 1755. The head start gave proprietors actual as well as symbolic power because their deputies drew up the original personal and commercial rolls, judging if an elderly peasant actually was 60 years old and free from the personal tax, or whether someone who made and sold a few sticks of furniture should come under the commercial tax. Hence the residents of the commune owed their very incorporation to the owners, whose senior position the Giunta announced most clearly.(126)

> For the formation of the rolls there must be a solemn convocation where everyone may speak and afterwards proceed to the proper election of the commercial and personal deputies. It is not meant however that the sentiments of the assembly will determine the composition of the rolls, which decision we assign to the justice of the property deputies and the final approval of the Giunta.

The law of 1755 omitted the above statement and apparently divided responsibility for the annual renewal of the rolls among all the deputies and an agent of the crown, but further instructions of September 1760 again revealed the basic desire for hierarchy. In exempting from the personal tax men with chronic illness and incapacity Milan bade the property deputies to use their ''conscience and sense of legality'' when deciding the facts of a case. They must also identify peasants on church lands to whom the concordat of 1757 had granted a one *lira* reduction in the tax, checking the applicant's testimony and evidence against their own knowledge and ''other secret information which they could obtain.''(127) More important the major act burdened personal and commercial deputies with blanket restrictions which undercut their specific and often incisive functions as adversaries. Attending the property convocations by right, they could vote only if they owned land and otherwise were ''merely to represent the interests of their electorate and register complaints for transmission to the royal government.'' Final remarks on the personal deputy then instructed him how to complain, summing up the paternal and suspicious attitude of the reformers toward the peasantry.(128)

> In all matters not mentioned above and not related to the affairs of those paying the personal tax, the personal deputy will have no reason to intervene nor will he have any voice. When some issue does require his intervention or opposition, he will state his views respectfully and

> without clamor or tumult, he will not initiate useless or captious
> litigation and he will accept with resignation the decisions which the
> tribunal declares to be just.

Indeed the attempt to restrain rural inhabitants did not end in 1755 as
we shall see when considering various amendments added to the
Censimento over the next ten years.

On the other hand the government never for a moment contemplated
leaving proprietors unsupervised in the enjoyment of their triumphs and
freedoms. Even as Neri and his colleagues weakend the authority of
peasant representatives, they carefully created a third regional force to
hem owners inside the land tax rules, forming the 1,492 communes
into 157 counties which became the jurisdictions of royal overseers
called chancellors *(regi cancelliere delegati)*.(129) These men put
residents and landlords under the "perpetual intelligence" of the crown
and hopefully defended them from private unsurpations, "especially
from anyone claiming tax exemptions."

> He must guide the execution of the present edict, not only with
> reference to his own duties, but also concerning the obligations of
> others in the commune. He will hinder transgressions of the act and
> inform the president of the Censimento of any serious problems.

Chancellors therefore had the assignment of preserving order in the
communes and enforcing old and new regulations about voting
procedures, the disposal of common lands and the conduct of elected or
appointed officials. They remained in close contact with Milan, attended
important meetings, validated all communal decisions and controlled
the precious maps and assessment rolls. They moved through the
district hearing complaints and talking with deputies; dissuaded the
latter from litigating with nearby communes over matters which could
be settled amicably; and brought to justice persons damaging the
commons. They also confronted Lombard feudalism in its last stage. By
tradition the *podestà* of an infeudated commune presided at general
assemblies in person or through an agent, but the Giunta abolished
substitution in these cases and required absentee feudal officers to accept
the chancellors as their spokesmen. If the *podestà* was resident and took
the chair, the chancellor stood beside him, advising participants of their
rights and those of the crown.(130) Meanwhile the chancellors were
themselves objects of government surveillance, a testing of their
competence and loyalty. "To avoid suspicion of partiality," they could
neither lease land nor accept economic commissions from proprietors of
the county, nor enter into any kind of private relationship with local
people. Naturally they could have no business dealings with the exactor.
The Giunta, which wanted chancellors experienced in public ad-

ministration and familiar with law or engineering, ordered them not to leave their districts even for short periods unless permitted, reviewed their work every three years and reserved the power of dismissing them at any time.

The chancellor, vigorous in the commune and obedient toward his superiors in Milan, was still no messenger of tyranny or strict absolutism. The reformers, judging communal politics incompatible with sound fiscal policy because the petty rural officials were corrupt themselves or unwilling accomplices for insubordinate nobles and ecclesiastics, intervened in the 1750s to discipline malefactors and ensure that both weak and strong paid their taxes. But they did not expect to burden the country-side with heavy government for long since they believed that soon the proper leaders of the land, the owners, would emerge and do for them the work of awarding justice. Hence they foresaw the day when the chancellor would be as much a servant of the commune as the crown.(131)

> For now the Giunta provides counties with chancellors who have the skills necessary for carrying the Censimento to conclusion. When vacancies occur after the law is executed, Her Majesty graciously will leave nominations for the respective communities.

The word "communities" meant for the Giunta only the property deputies of a given district who would meet under the chairmanship of a temporary chancellor sent from Milan and vote on candidates after discussing their qualifications. The name of the person with majority support would go to the crown for approval. Moreover from the beginning, even before they participated in his appointment, the communes paid the chancellor's salary. Pietro Verri once gave this fact as one of the four major weaknesses of the Censimento, arguing that a chancellor never should feel any financial obligation toward owners because he was so often engaged in protecting communes from these same men.(132) Obviously the Giunta members saw things differently: they feared covert exchanges between chancellors and individual owners; but doubted that landlords in their public and corporate capacity, once getting from the census law a new system of representation and a new set of interests, would coerce an official whom they had chosen and who administered a tax of considerable benefit to them. Much later Carli reported that Neri was unhappy with the method of paying chancellors and would have preferred a uniform salary derived from general funds. However the comment which he added for himself and probably for Neri showed how little his thoughts were on any deep conflict pitting chancellors against owners. The problem, he wrote, was that mountain people had little money for the chancellor who exhausted himself just keeping in touch with the communes of his district, "whereas in the plains owners of latifundia are rich and allot large stipends to chancellors with easy work and few expenses."(133) Likewise in September of 1760 Governor Firmian, after lamenting the poor quality of many chancellors, which he blamed on low salaries, told Vienna that proprietors quickly discovered the value of expert supervisors and now were asking for better men.(134) At the beginning of the year he had tried to obtain a favorable reception for the chancellors in their new districts by advising them "to use all caution, decorum and moderation in treating with property deputies and other communal representatives."(135) The next month, February 1760, he learned that chancellors and owners were quarreling, and his tone became harsh: (136)

> His Excellency orders chancellors to moderate their behavior toward communities as toward proprietors. He will tolerate neither perversity from owners nor excess from chancellors.

This document speaks for itself about the chancellor's tenuous position amid the crown and the landed classes.

The wide ranging transformation of communal government did not exhaust Giunta plans for remaking political and administrative institutions in Lombardy. The scientific measurement of agricultural wealth eliminated fiscal distinctions between rural and civil owners, previously an open invitation for the latter to cut their taxes, but the political machinery employed by cities to win and exploit privileges remained and could serve corrupt ends again. Therefore to safeguard his modern country regimes from archaic instruments of urban power Neri moved the struggle for the cadaster into the municipalities, bringing the whole society under his purview.(137) Unfortunately his leverage was slight in the second setting, perhaps because no important groups favored changing intramural politics, and so he left undisturbed the oligarchic agencies which supervised guilds or controlled crucial city affairs like victualing and sanitation.(138) Instead the Giunta defined a new realm of "general administration" for the joint concern of capitals and provinces, including real taxes, troop quartering and sometimes the city budget itself. Provincial governments dissolved and their work fell to special metropolitan committees composed of urban leaders (decurions) and territorial landowners. The innovation, limited in scope, was also limited in detail, since the reformed committees had to cooperate periodically with the patrician councils which dominated city life; and the provincial representatives, though they could not be decurions, that is concurrent members of the ancient councils, could be patricians out of office, as were the first four deputies chosen in Milan's *Ducato*.(139) Nonetheless contemporaries could appreciate the attempt to resolve a major problem in Lombardy, the fact that ruling families in provincial capitals formulated policies injurious to the rest of the country and then felt the effects only through a filter of privileges which drew individual benefit from universal misfortune. Carli ignored the law's willingness to sanction many advantages of a class which he mistrusted, and applauded the introduction into provincial-city government of men well disposed toward the country-side.(140)

> Without establishing a union of the tax payers in a single corps it would not have been possible to stop the abuses caused by the separation of rural and civil. Nor could anyone have proclaimed more effectively the need for a perfectly uniform society between city and province than through the consolidation of common interests and the ending of those separate jurisdictions which for so long fed the discords and conspired to the ruin of public and private life.

Equally favorable was the judgment of Verri in old age, though since the 1760s he had come to value some privileges of the patriciate as a check on ministerial despotism. Around 1795 he recalled that with the advent of provincial deputies in the cities "representation became legitimate."(141) Even the person most disturbed by the inadequacy of urban reform, Francesco Carpani, generally assumed that the land tax was secure, and focused his attention on the internal administration of Milan. In an essay of 1771 he complained that a small circle of nobles, the decurions, still had far too much say in the city, profitting from the high price of necessities which they themselves engendered through consumption duties and monopolies. Indeed this situation, besides making the revival of commerce and manufacturing in Lombardy an impossibility, was also a threat to agriculture, as history had shown, but Carpani thought it more likely that the success of the Censimento in stimulating cultivation eventually would encourage the crown to attack the patricians in their last stronghold and give the metropolis the same kind of honest regulation already enjoyed by the commune.(142)

Certainly the concessions of the Giunta in the cities were not serious enough to deflect or vitiate the main thrust of the reform movement. The selection system for provincial representatives extended the authority of the Censimento just as it permitted deferential electors to uphold patrician leadership. Usually the communal property deputies of a given district cast the primary ballots, finding candidates among landlords with property in the locality and assessments in the whole province which exceeded values appropriate for the size and wealth of jurisdiction: 6,000 *scudi* in Cremona, 4,000 in Pavia, 2,000 in Como.

So the formal qualifications for the office were ownership of land listed on tax rolls making no reference to social ranks, and the favor of men who participated in local and territorial government because they were *estimati,* taxpayers in good standing with the census law. Moreover the decurions themselves, the patricians as patricians, felt the need for conforming with the standards of background which provincial representatives brought to the committees of general administration, since they could not go from their protected councils to the senior level of government unless they had as much real income as their ''rural'' colleagues. This requirement to keep up economically also pushed patricians toward acceptance of the Censimento by the proviso that rich owners were ineligible for provincial posts if they claimed a fiscal exemption which the crown contested or which was worth more than half their total tax bill. The Cremonese act applying property qualifications directly to the patrician council stated the Giunta position with special clarity.

> Being just that the general council unite the most conspicuous part of those concerned with the payment of public tribute, persons who have in the province a smaller assessment than 6,000 *scudi* cannot be elected decurions . . . Decurions losing their qualifications after election will enjoy honorary prerogatives only . . . Those with exemptions in litigation or surpassing half their taxes cannot be elected decurions, and if already elected, they likewise will abstain from voting.

In sum Neri departed from his program and recognized the hereditary urban nobility as a legal caste, but he did so in a way that could make the patricians behave more like other large landowners in Lombardy, whose sway rested on affluence and culture rather than privilege. It was not a bad compromise given the aim of the reformers to create an energetic ruling elite which acquired new talents without losing the old, which obeyed the laws while preserving the aristocratic trait of serving the public easily and well. Their intention was neither to break the North Italian tradition of government emanting from cities nor to fill important offices with country bumpkins. Instead they sought a blend of urban and rural values so that men living in the metropolis or familiar with its civilization would use power with good sense precisely because their prominence was openly and almost mathematically related to agriculture. The Giunta expressed this ideal in the attributes which it demanded from provincial representatives in addition to riches.(143)

> This person . . . must be of good character and honest family, have an education far from any mechanical trade and possess the cultivation necessary to inform himself of public affairs and treat them with the prudence suitable for an assembly of the whole province.

The Enlightenment, one might generalize, wished to liberate men by weakening the city as a monopoly corporation and simultaneously infusing the country-side with civic virtue. The municipal reforms lasted from January of 1756 to February of 1758 as one after another the six capitals and provinces got fresh charters. Cremona, the first, was a kind of show place, the model which the Giunta would have followed in the rest of the country under more favorable conditions. Here the patrician council itself became the agency of general administration and consequently submitted to great changes in composition and structure. The old members, sitting without term on account of their standing in the city, lost the vote unless they had real assessments of 6,000 *scudi;* and accepted as colleagues sixteen wealthy provincial representatives, new decurions who received life mandates from the communal property deputies. The council then drew from its reconstituted membership a ten man executive committee, the Congregation of Prefects, which contained at least two patrician legal experts *(dottori di collegio)*, two provincial representatives and two guild deputies, the latter because four guildsmen already sat with the decurions, a special feature of Cremonese politics. The council, either in full session or through its executive, cared for a city-province budget and the land tax; it also selected, again from its own ranks, two representatives to the Congregation of State, a patrician orator and a provincial syndic, as well as a local syndic whose job was to meet with the prefects and "sustain the cause of the rural plebians and especially the poor agriculturalists." Naturally enough the crown held the right, in this charter and all the others, to approve or reject most decisions, including elections. Outside Cremona the Giunta relied on working committees to make reforms, keeping away from decurion councils except in Lodi and Casal Maggiore where it established property qualifications for them.(144) In Pavia there was a congregation of general administration which assembled twenty-four members in the following manner: the patrician council sent four decurions and two legal experts; the twelve richest owners in the province supplied four delegates picked by lot from their number; and communal property deputies in fourteen county districts nominated three persons for each jurisdiction, leaving the final choice to the Giunta and later to the congregation. The assessment limit was 4,000 *scudi,* the term in office four years, and no constituency could select someone who already was speaking for another. The congregation was responsible for provincial finances while the decurion council, sometimes involved in the latter sphere, controlled a separate city budget. These bodies together chose a patrician orator, and the congregation alone elected two syndics. In Casal Maggiore the decurion council, limited to patricians with assessments of 2,000 *scudi,* named all four members of the small committee for general administration: one person from the law college, one free choice, presumedly a decurion, and two representatives from the group of eighteen richest owners in the province. Serving two year terms, they were unusually dependent upon the decurion council in their management of the land tax and a city-province budget. The law let the decurions select their orator and made no mention of syndics. Como was divided into two parts. In the urban division, the capital and four neighboring districts, the patrician council chose four decurions and one legal expert for the committee of general administration, and the district property deputies elected four representatives. The decurions on the committee needed an assessment of 3,000 *scudi,* district representatives 2,000, and all members served for life. The council must have named the orator, though there was no special provision for him. Rural Como had a separate budget and administration, the responsibility of a twelve man governing committee reflecting the wishes and interests of nine districts. In each district the property deputies elected for life one or two representatives from among the twelve richest owners of the area. The committee chose its syndics "according to custom." Officers from the two sections of Como met once a year to discuss joint expenditures, probably small sums, and in case of dispute the crown was arbiter. The congregation of prefects in Lodi included two decurions and six other owners who came in pairs from the capital, the country-side and the city of Milan. The patrician council, with its own assessment minimum of 4,000 *scudi,* appointed the decurions; the non-decurions were chosen by their respective constituents, the non-patrician owners of Lodi city, and so on. The non-patrician electors possessed property worth over 1,000 *scudi,* their candidates 4,000. During their four year terms the prefects had considerable freedom from the decurion council in administering real taxes and a city-province budget. The orator was nominated by the congregation and approved by the council; two syndics were elected at a convocation of rural owners. In Milan ten out of sixteen members on the committee for general administration properly represented the local nobility: four decurions, two legal experts, two urban syndics and two high city officers, the Vicario of Provision and the Tenente Regio, all chosen in one way or another, at one time or another, by the patrician Council of Sixty. The six remaining members, even if patricians, were associated with the province: four men who owed their selection to the first (richest) deputies in the communes, and two syndics carried over from the old

Ducato government. However after the election of 1758 the committee, on the advice of the patrician council, coopted provincial deputies as vacancies occurred; and when the two provincial syndics died they were not replaced. The Vicario of Provision and the Tenente Regio sat on the committee because of their offices, the decurions, legal experts and provincial deputies had four year terms, and the syndics were life members. The assessment limit for everyone was 6,000 *scudi*. The Council of Sixty, which elected its orator as usual, and the committee collaborated in tending Censimento affairs and a city-province budget, though at first the wealthy patrician Bank of Santo Ambrogio was independent.

Evidently the Giunta itself was unsure in this maze of councils and committees how to achieve maximum protection for the provinces without exploding the wrath of the oligarchs, and sometimes its expedients were dubious. Thus the discredited system of administering real taxes according to the location of owners, not properties, survived in Lodi where territorial representatives contended with delegates from Milan as well as their own patricians. Yet the reformers probably did all that was possible in the cities and got no thanks for their moderation from the habitual enemies of the Censimento. The leaders of Milan, forgetting their special privileges in Lodi and at home, complained bitterly about the loss of influence in Pavia. They owned much land in this province and normally enjoyed commensurate power through the *Congregazione degli interessati milanesi,* which the Giunta had abolished. Now indeed a few Milanese sat on the Pavian committee of general administration as representatives for districts or rich owners — the simple residence requirement being a domicile anywhere in Lombardy — but they could not take a major position because of absenteeism, and supposedly they spoke for local constituents rather than the national capital. After hearing arguments the Giunta agreed that Milan had suffered a loss and allowed its agents to check the financial records in Pavia annually. Otherwise an edict of 1 October 1757 ordered "literal" obedience for the Pavian charter, "imposing silence on all pretentions of the Milanese owners for a separate congregation or for preponderance on the existing general congregation of taxpayers."(145) The municipal reforms, despite many flaws, were worth defending afterall.

While still occupied with the cities the Neri Giunta began its final series of political actions, amending the law of 1755 for twenty towns, unified districts and oversized communities which needed more complex institutions than the villages. The changes were not simply adjustments

of scale since almost every new government made wealth instead of
ownership the basic qualification for citizenship, depriving small
proprietors of rights given them by the original legislation. The act of 19
August 1757 creating a single administration for the district of Varese
announced the trend.(146)

> In conformity with said unification there must be one convocation of
> possessors which will consolidate the representation of the public and
> the faculty to dispose of common matters . . . And because the good of
> all requires that public affairs be committed to those who have the
> most conspicuous interest in them; and because, on the other hand,
> the tumultuous meeting of little owners would bring forth confusion
> and disruption: therefore the convocation will be composed solely of
> those who hold in the district property assessed at 600 *scudi* or more.

The exact wording of the second sentence was used in the charters for
Monza and Triviglio, and its spirit shaped fifteen others. Moreover
twelve of the jurisdictions imposed social as well as financial
requirements on some officers, who had to be respectable and
cultivated, never rustic, mechanical or servile.(147) Legislators applied
these rules mostly to substitutes with low assessment qualifications, no
doubt assuming that wealthier principals would always live in the proper
fashion, though in three communities the deputies and councilmen were
also affected. At the same time non-propertied deputies disappeared
from the Ordinary Council of Abiate-Grasso and the Council General of
Canzo, where they had maintained seats contrary to the communal
reform. Altogether the amended governments allowed poor subjects,
landed or not, to participate only through personal and commercial
deputies working under disabilities as in the village assemblies.(147A)

Next after dealing with the people the Giunta turned to the opposite
end of the social structure, the hereditary ruling families which existed
in about half the twenty communities as minor patriciates. They kept
their elite status, indeed one aim of the amendments was to protect it,
but in the context of the Censimento. In eight regions, mostly without
towns *(borghi),* modern councils took ever from old ones the members
whose surveyed land was sufficient to establish financial eligibility. Such
councilors enjoyed, besides proprietary powers from the law of 1755, all
traditional rights and privileges that were not ''repugnant to the present
tax system.'' Usually they held their posts for life, unless assessments
fell below the limit, and filled vacancies by cooption. Four charters
mentioned specifically that the office was personal and non-heritable.
The towns of Monza, Varese and Triviglio, like the cities, were
separate entites in their territories. Inside Monza the ancient Council of
Sixty governed as always, its life members satisfying only the

requirements of their own statutes and choosing similarly qualified replacements. However before embarking upon costly projects the council needed permission from taxpayers with assessments over 500 *scudi* supervising the Censimento in the territorial convocation. The regents of Varese, six men handling town affairs, perhaps were not patricians because they came on three year terms from the district assembly. But while in office they had customary honors and privileges, and indication of oligarchy in other charters, and the demand that they be residents may have insured their suitable rank. They too worked in subordination to the convocation on tax questions. Arrangements for Triviglio were less equivocal and show best how the reform operated. The parent convocation, joining owners worth 600 *scudi* or more, elected from its roll sixteen residents to found anew the town agency known as the Regency Council or Council of Provision. Here are the relevant instructions.(148)

> With reference to the said Regency the so-called Association of Vicinanza *(il Corpo così detto della Vicinanza)* has exclusive rights *(privativa ragione)*, as do certain families recognized by the town for particular merit; thus in case one finds in the said association and families individuals with the qualities previously noted, we wish and order that such individuals receive preference in the election ... Those chosen will continue in office for life if the necessary quantity of assessment endures, and when there is a vacancy the same Council of Sixteen will discover persons who have the above requisites.

In this way the Giunta, firm and generous toward the upper classes, paternal and correct toward the peasantry, spread its political program through the cities, towns and country-side of Lombardy.

When Neri modified the communal law for the special jurisdictions he accepted the advice and encouragement of local people. Eighteen charters stated that the communities had "implored" the Giunta to help them reach an accommodation with the general regulations. This raises the possibility that the amendments signified the first intervention in Lombard politics of the new social forces stemming from the Censimento. Indeed four charters ascribed requests for assistance and suggestions for action to the property deputies, officers functioning only since the preliminary edict of April 1753. So the Giunta change of heart about the role of peasants in the convocation may have originated with substantial owners just beginning to explore the land tax mechanisms. After 1760 several communities petitioned the crown to increase the entrance requirements of their assemblies, and probably similar proposals were made in the earlier period.(149) Anyway the charters demonstrated the basis for such activity, ten of them offering information on the movement of rural notables out of obscurity into the hierarchy of reform. The act for Triviglio told the absentee first deputy to pick as a substitute "a resident of respectability and cultivation, at least a minor owner, excluding always persons of mechanical or servile condition." While in Gravedona:

> As nearly all the major taxpayers of the territory are permanent residents, the three with the largest assessments must be among the number of the twelve councilors, so long as they . . . are cultivated and capable persons.

Some of these men undoubtedly were established leaders, the patricians used to office as a birthright, but not all. The Castel-Leone charter, without reference to oligarchic institutions or groups, envisioned a pool of thirty-six resident owners, assessed at over 700 *scudi*, neither rustic nor mechanical, who would provide nominees for the eighteen member general council.(150) The country-side therefore contained the land-lords sought by the Giunta, individuals fit for political work in an aristocratic society, yet apart from the privileged corporations which hindered financial improvement. Hopefully they would respond to modern ideas and opportunities, uplifting the state after a century of stagnation.

The amendment for Soresina, dated 22 February 1758, completed the political reforms of the second Giunta, which dissolved on 14 April. It is clear that the communal, town and metropolitan charters were all secondary or supporting instruments of the fiscal law, intended before everything else to gain the crown obedience and income. Yet they were also genuinely liberal acts whose authors believed as a matter of principle that taxpayers deserved a measure of control over the collection, administration and disbursement of their own money. The charters for Cremona and Varese typically stated that the founding of proprietary councils and convocations was in accordance with simple justice as well as expediency, and a decade later Neri, in discussing Tuscan practices, repeated the argument.(151)

> The Magistrate of the Nine wields an indiscreet despotism in the cities and communities of the country, using every occasion to withdraw rights from the latter and arrogate for itself the power to decide the most minute affairs, which are better handled by local representatives. The Magistrate thus tramples upon norms of decency and good economy, upon the rule that he who pays the tribute must receive all possible satisfaction.

Moreover the Hapsburg ministers, though servants of absolutism, understood that their creations needed some spontaneous support, and they saw in a purified system of public representation the means by which owners could and would defend the census. In 1760 Governor Firmian, outraged at the Provisional Commission for reducing the assessments of Milanese nobles, wrote to Kaunitz that the culprits. (152)

> are much criticized in the communes where the big proprietors executing the tax show their friendship for it and their disrelish of the old ways.

In such light one may properly evaluate a passage in the *Progress Report* supposedly summing up Neri's attitude toward the Congregation of State: partly ironic and scornful, it nonetheless contained an important element of truth.(153)

> Attacking the prerogatives of the Congregation is no plan of the Giunta. Its wish is rather to amplify and strengthen the duties of this body, today a collection of provincial attorneys who lack any serious mandate. The Giunta wishes to make the Congregation more respectable than it is . . . giving it the aids which it requires . . . to protect the public patrimony . . . No longer obliged, as they are now, to stand by as idle spectators of disorder . . . the representatives will have an authority commensurate with their just zeal for ameliorating the situation.

The parochial and dependent assemblies of the Censimento never gave landowners the broad and secure liberties of feudal privilege or 19th century self-government, but they did provide them with status and leverage which went beyond the mere right of due process in a "legal despotism."(154)

Indeed at the very end of the old regime in Italy the communal and provincial reforms of the 1750s inspired Pietro Verri in his attempt to devise a scheme for constitutional monarchy capable of helping Lombardy ride out the revolutionary storm.(155) When in the spring of 1790 Emperor Leopold asked his subjects how he could reduce the tensions caused by his autocratic brother, Verri replied that henceforth he must rule through a series of fundamental statutes which he and his ministers would legislate and enforce only on the advice of a permanent representative assembly. In explaining what he meant he referred again and again to the Censimento as the exemplary code which had done much good, involved many errors and was still the potential mainspring of the whole society. After putting an end to the manipulations of powerful owners and corrupt representatives, a great step forward, the census gradually had drifted in the opposite direction, becoming the tool of despotic royal ministers and officials, so that, finally, a commune could not build an oven without waiting endlessly for permission from Milan. Reversing his earlier contention about the chancellor, Verri now berated the crown, especially under Joseph, for transforming this one-time servant of the commune into a meddlesome agent of the central government, ''no longer elected by the community, nor even paid by it.'' Hence it was necessary to return to the original aims of the reform: a royal tribunal would prevent communes and provinces from reducing the tax rolls, either by granting owners unwarranted exemptions or by impoverishing them through the contraction of heavy local debts; all else would be the domain of the law and the taxpayers. As determined in the act, property deputies and convocations would regulate the economy of the communes, municipal and territorial deputies would do the same for the provinces, and members of the Congregation of State would take care of general expenditures. The mode of elections, duration of office and method of making decisions likewise would follow the legislation of thirty years before, no less than the selection and functioning of the chancellor, chosen by the communities which he served. However the work of correction and restoration could have little value without the addition of a major novelty, the establishment of a representative assembly for all Lombardy which would keep watch over the organic laws and advise the monarch in advance whether any changes subsequently introduced from Vienna were acceptable to the country. Verri's insistence on the last point, which did not arise naturally out of the achievements or dreams of Neri and his colleagues, was a sign, as he said, that a new day had dawned, and that men must take account of the upheavals in progress around them. On the other hand the land tax remained the indispensable foundation upon which Verri built his parliament, not only because its technical facilities would be of use, but also because it had already identified the likely guardians of the constitution, the *estimati* or notables who could assume leadership at a time when the claims of traditional nobility were in ill repute.

> We have a cadaster: the possessors divide themselves into equal masses; every community in a mass selects its deputies, who meet in the local town where they name their public representative; these nominees form the (central) assembly of the state.

At the same time, logically enough, Milan's Council of Sixty would loosen its exclusive connection with the patriciate and become the organ of all resident landowners, fulfilling the promise of the Cremonese charter of 1756. Perhaps too the fact that Verri made the constitutional assembly mostly consultative and left the initiative with the sovereign was another link between his program and Neri's. Though the amount of liberty and autonomy that he wanted for Lombardy probably would have shocked the Tuscan, neither of them thought of the country as other than a satellite of some mighty outside power, the recipient of protection and guidance in the large affairs of Europe. Instead they hoped for a political and administrative order which would let them exercise their talents freely and effectively in the daily tasks of domestic enlightenment. In this limited context the laws would rule first, then, in varying degree, the judgement of notables like themselves. In either case the ideals and even the details of the Censimento would set standards of conduct, as Verri fervently proposed.

By such maxims will be organized the municipal councils, and in such a manner the permanent public bodies, with successive and temporary members, will be set up; and, adhering to the census reform, the province (of Lombardy) will receive a stable legal form, subject to a humane and enlightened monarch, who will have assured it forever against the evil provincial despotism which has degraded and oppressed it.

CHAPTER V

THE TAX IN OPERATION

The two not entirely compatible aims of the land tax were to make Lombardy a duitful and productive part of the Hapsburg empire, and to free its people from the real and supposed confusions, constraints and corruptions of a traditional society. This conclusion derives chiefly from a consideration of the reform in the period of its construction between 1718 and 1760, and hopefully the preceding narrative and analysis have rendered it both meaningful and persuasive, but it may also be elucidated and sustained by a brief examination of the completed system during the early years of its operation. A historical epilog offers the further advantage of confirming that the Censimento had an actuality distinct from the paper descriptions of it in the legislation. With the tax safely launched, Vienna still needed to give it a reliable central direction which, unlike the Temporary Commission, would never favor one group over another, especially at the expense of the crown, and to ensure that it functioned in the field as the law demanded. For several years nothing was done about the former problem while Maria Theresa's ministers concentrated on the war, then on their plans for increasing or extending royal control over urban business and over the administration of indirect taxes, which, through the farming of duties on salt, tobacco, powder and the movement of goods, brought in around 4.6 million *lira* annually.(156) Only in November of 1765 did they establish in Milan a Supreme Economic Council with authority to supervise the land tax and the *mercimonio* in the same way as the Neri Giunta; to enforce and improve laws governing guilds and commercial transactions; to recommend changes in the methods of marketing grain; and to see that the new Mixed Farm honored the provision in its contract assigning the crown a one third voice in its councils.(157) In fact no single agency could accomplish so much, and above all it could not carve out for itself such a large place in the life of the capital city, where, as we know from Carpani, the patricians loomed as powerful as ever in 1771. However since the concluding passage of the November edict assumed the resistance of these nobles, or at least of their most prestigious officers, and condemned it without a hearing, the political intention undoubtedly was to defend the census from them and to mount an attack on their local institutions.(158)

> Finally Her Majesty prohibits every complaint, remonstrance or brief which directly or indirectly opposes the things expressed above; and with Her Sovereign Royal Power absolutely deprives the Senate of any faculty whatsoever to annotate, interpret or modify this present royal constitution, the full and entire execution and observation of which she wishes and commands.

On the first of November the president-designate of the Economic Council, Gianrinaldo Carli, told his cousin, Giuseppe Gravisi, that he soon would be at odds with the Senate, "which until now has been the only supreme council."(159)

Though Carli lacked administrative experience he was otherwise well fitted to manage the Censimento without regard for the special interests and claims of the Milanese patriciate, and in general to challenge this group whenever he had the support and encouragement of Vienna. Like Neri he was a foreigner, born in 1720 in Capodistria, the capital of a Venetian province. At home he was a member of the dominant oligarchy, a count proud of his nobility, yet he disliked privilege and aristocratic government, advocating instead the kind of regime in which an absolute prince ruled and vigorous gentlemen were free to serve, not to oppose or live as parasites. When a student of nineteen he organized his friends into a historical society called *l'Accademia degli operosi,* thus distinguishing it from the existing association in Capodistria which gathered only for ceremony and display. A lifelong scholar, he became professor of astronomy and nautical science at the University of Padua in 1744 immediately upon completing his education there; seven years later he resigned, weary of the low salary — he was not a rich man — and wishing to investigate subjects "of greater use in society." Before long he was a noted expounder of monetary history and policy, and with the publication of his voluminous *Delle moneta* from 1754 onward various Italian leaders began to consider him as a possible adviser and official. State employment was just what the author wanted and to announce his readiness he visited Tuscany, Piedmont and Lombardy, staying three years in Milan where he met Neri and conversed with him about the evolving tax reform.(160) Not finding a post that pleased him Carli returned to Capodistria and during the period 1756-64 personally supervised the farms and wool factory of his inheritance, attempting to make the latter profitable while improving his lands by careful marketing and the introduction of new crops. For a time he continued the endeavor from Milan, in the fall of 1765 sending Giuseppe Gravisi a book on sericulture with the comment that owners should study agronomy and increase their revenues. Eighteen months later, fully occupied with Lombard affairs, he wrote to Giuseppe, "it is almost March and we must think of planting. I won't be satisfied unless I have 1,000 mulberry schrubs and at least 1,000 fruit trees."(161) Naturally he rejected the notion of derogation as false and absurd, merely an excuse for "gothic indolence." The nobles, he suggested in early 1765, already bought and sold agricultural land and products, and there was no reason why they should neglect commerce and manufacturing which were more lucrative for a nation than farming.(162)

Carli's business experience also affected his view of politics, causing or stimulating deep hostility toward the ancient constitution of Capodistria. The city and its environs, each with a population of about 5,000, were ruled by a small closed corporation of families whose right to be represented on the Major Council supposedly predated the 14th century. A few of the councilors possessed impressive titles like marchese or count, and a few more enjoyed the bare style of *Nobilità*, but most of them were humble fishermen and farmers known as "citizens." All the other residents, the vast majority, no matter how genteel and financially independent, were excluded from office and labeled "popular." By the mid-18th century the very presence of the "citizens" at meetings was a topic for mockery, and since their rivalry with the nobles prevented the formation of strong public policies, the whole arrangement verged on collapse. The Venetian overlords, themselves oligarchs, were hardly qualified to break the deadlock, and their agents joined rather than resolved factional fights.(163) Indeed Carli might easily have been as complacent as most of the Venetians, for he belonged to the upper nobility, and his friend and cousin, Marchese Girolamo Gravisi, Giuseppe's brother, was a powerful man in the community. Nonetheless his ire was aroused exceedingly by the gradual failure of his wool finishing plant, which he blamed on the local and sovereign magistrates, paying little attention to his own mistakes and difficulties beyond anyone's control. Obscure complaints to his cousins about road construction and flooding conveyed clearly enough his hurt disappointment that the factory, "errected and maintained by a citizen who had no other wish than to promote the welfare and honor of his fatherland," never recieved "special tutelage and protection" from the city. When in November of 1764, the textile operation nearly in ruins, he left home to teach at the University of Piacenza and maneuver for a high position in Lombardy, his feelings were bitter toward the government.(164)

Too painful is this parting from you (Girolamo Gravisi) and my few friends in the city which grudges a citizen who has never had another thought than through his work to procure for it all honor and advantage. I must bury quickly the pain of separation and the consciousness of universal ingratitude.

In 1770 Carli provided a more comprehensive and detached judgement about politics in Capodistria, occasioned by a crisis there, and perhaps enriched by knowledge of the Milanese situation which he had acquired in the meantime. Between 1769 and 1771 the "people," with the help of some dissident nobles, pressed their demands for a place on the council, and the Venetian *podestà,* partly agreeing and partly fearing "those strange resolutions of which the popular imagination is capable," advised his superiors to impose reforms. Instead the republic supported the status quo, firmly and astutely, ending the struggle with minor concessions. Carli, congratulating Giuseppe Gravisi on his escape from the "disgrace" of living under "victorious plebians," rejoiced at the defeat of the popular party which he suspected of mysterious evil designs. On the other hand he realized that the oligarchic constitution was "odious and obsolete," and desired positive action from Venice. The only solution, he insisted, was to enlarge the council's executive committee, generally thought of as an instrument of cliquish control, and to increase the number of noble families.(165)

Carli learned in Capodistria and elsewhere that patrician leaders were too tired and selfish either to assist a fellow aristocrat with ambitions for modern development or to forestall popular insurrection. They therefore must become a service nobility, accepting the authority of a prince who would stand above them, and the association of gentlemen who without feudal or municipal titles and privileges led noble, cultivated and productive lives, and who now would stand beside them. That at least was the conception of politics and society which Carli worked out in literary form in the 1770s. His *l'Uomo libero,* conceived in 1765 and finished in 1776, began with the argument that government originated in the defense of private property, and that natural differences among individuals produced an unequal division of land, separating the population into owners and agricultural laborers. The inferiority and servitude of the later were inevitable and reasonable since they would starve if they could not till the farms of their betters. Carli then invoked a negative assessment of social dynamics to explain that the proper relationship between landlords and peasants constantly broke down because the excessive greed and ambition of the rich and the hopeless envy of the poor made class war endemic and interminable. Escape from the impasse came with the establishment of monarchy, the unique institution capable of mastering property and inequality, the necessary and dangerous concomitants of civilization.

> The society admitting property and freedom of contract will suffer the corruption of its members and search for a remedy, which is the sovereign.

Even so the monarch needed assistance in keeping tensions at a tolerable level, and it was essential to supplement royal pacification with the legal designation of social classes, which would assure everyone that his condition, duties and rights had the sanction of law and furthered public good rather than being the result of coercion or private will. Each class would serve the others, the little people enjoying the free employment of their industry while "the rich and the nobles" found the glory they sought in the offices of religion and justice. The administrative corps simultaneously would follow the instructions of the sovereign and register the complaints of the nation, engendering in the best circumstances liberty, order and contentment. Though Carli was clear that the nobles exercised civil rather than patrimonial authority, he gave no details about their provenance or internal gradations, using interchangeably the words *ricchi, nobili, grandi, illustri*.(166) However in an essay on education published in 1774 he indicated that no one should obtain a place of command simply by pulling himself up out of the masses, the selfmade man tending more to undermine than stabilize communities.(167)

> Hence a society composed of various classes cannot have a uniform education; because between the great (*grandi*) and the people there is an infinite distance; and the middle classes (*classe di mezzo*) which unite the two extremes increase the difficulty (of devising uniform education). Supposing that persons of wisdom and learning administer the republic, if the people have the supreme power to decide then . . . party or chance actually will rule, never mature counsel. So much the worse when, as must happen, the middle classes between the wise (*sapienti*) and the people teem with half-educated, determined, fanatical, false, malevolent, interested and vain men, of which the world is never under provided.

Altogether the elites in *l'Uomo libero* and *Nuovo metodo per le scuole pubbliche di Italia* remind one of Neri's civil nobility, and especially of the ideal representatives of the Censimento communal reform law who, pushing aside the rough entrepreneurs of the country-side and resisting the magnates of the city, would "be of good character and honest family, have an education far from any mechanical trade and possess the cultivation necessary to inform (themselves) of public affairs."(168)

It is true that the ideas just canvassed did not match every action taken by Carli while head of the land tax, for he was a complex and contradictory person, but generally he moved in their direction, at times under strict orders from the crown, which oddly made his total career more consistent than he himself might have wished. On the aim of reducing patrician power he never wavered, as Neri predicted when in February of 1766 he told him that his "firmness, energy and control" were exactly the qualities needed to protect the census from the kind of "vandals" who had almost subverted it in 1758.(169) Indeed for several years the Economic Council and the nobles of the capital fought over questions of policy and jurisdiction, and though Carli was not victorious, neither did he yield any ground. During the summer and fall of 1766 he and Kaunitz anxiously watched the rise of food prices in Milan, both convinced that the municipal government by remaining inactive hoped to discredit them and their programs. Carli assumed that the urban masses would blame the wrong officials for their ills because "the nobility which has so many rights of the crown encourages discontent toward royal regulations in order to appear as the champion of the people, who therefore complain . . . only in accordance with the wishes and opinions of the nobles." The minister replied:

> It is absolutely necessary . . . that daily prices do not alter greatly in prejudice of popular needs, and since the (Milanese) Tribunal of Provision gives excuses instead of looking for solutions, the Economic Council must double its efforts to hold the civic administration accountable.

The Vicario of Provision, for his part, claimed precedence over Carli in matters of mutual concern, and refused to send him information about the city budget as the Censimento rules required. The Senate also demanded respect for its dignity and authority, with Carli countering that the sovereign assigned and denied functions and honors as she saw fit. In March of 1767 the exasperated president of the Economic Council informed Vienna that Milan's city-province executive committee as well as the Congregation of State, "whose leader is the Vicario of Provision," had not yet supplied him with receipts and other financial documents for 1765; and a few months later he added that the scrupulous attention which he and his colleagues bestowed on even the smallest communal expenditure could not produce maximum benefits for the state so long as the capital and the Congregation retained their autonomy.(170)

By now Carli felt near hatred for the patricians, comparing them with a patient who suffered from "exhaustion, bad physical habits and profound sickness," and was incapable of responding soon to the medicine of reform.(171) In March of 1768 he sent Kaunitz a secret essay on the situation in Lombardy which contained a historical introduction showing how the many had endured the ''greediness of the few.''(172) Spanish rule was a failure, he wrote, for the reason that Charles V and his successors, while strong in their possession of the province, never overcame or reversed the basic loss of executive authority that occurred between 1499 and 1525 when the Milanese nobles, and among them the most wealthy and mighty, captured the Senate, the office of Vicario of Provision, formerly a ducal agent, and the General Council, whose membership fell from 150 to 60. Afterward the oligarchs, satisfying their ambition and avarice independently of public good, led Spanish governors into a morass of bad aministrative practices which crippled the state finances and finally caused the huge bankruptcy of 1668. In this way Carli uncovered the source of pre-Austrian decadence, working himself into a tirade.(173)

> At first the observer will marvel that in the midst of common misery the city of Milan has kept its splendor, and the nobility has gained honors . . . luxury and eminence . . . Thus whoever turns his eyes from the nation to only the elevated and restricted sphere of nobles and landlords becomes dazzled and also deluded. Whereas the politically acute person who penetrates to causes before deciding on the worth and reality of effects . . . will see that all power and riches had been concentrated in the hands of a few whose prosperity was born precisely in popular misery, the one growing in proportion with the other . . . So the city of Milan and its nobility acquired crown rights and formed a sort of dominion over the people who now regarded themselves as subject to a force other than their true and natural sovereign. I do not know where such a system might have ended, though it has the potential for a stupendous revolution, and I am sure than men holding many royal prerogatives cannot be docile or subordinate.

A fascinating glimpse into the heated atmosphere which induced Carli to write these lines comes from Pietro Verri who over time upheld both sides of the debate. As late as January of 1768 he still looked forward to the day when the Milanese would discover that their patrician leaders, false patriots, had insterted themselves between the people and the sovereign only to usurp and abuse power.(174) Gradually this attitude changed, as did more rapidly his admiration and friendship for Carli, of whom he first spoke harshly in February of 1768.(175) In June of 1768, and again in July of 1769, he heard fragmentary reports of Carli's secret essay and immediately judged it a threat to Lombardy because its glowing description of prosperity under Austrian rule might convince Vienna that taxes could be raised and that protests from natives reflected a quarrelsome and recalcitrant spirit rather than legitimate grievances. He suspected that Carli praised the wisdom of the imperial government with such exaggeration as a means of advancing himself, and that he was in some kind of conspiratorial league with the great tax farmer Antonio

Greppi, who wanted to show that the economy suffered no damage from
his fiscal operations.(176) Verri soon believed that a vast plot was under
way, partly financial and partly political, which involved Carli, Carpani,
Greppi, Firmian, Stefano Lottinger, a member of the Economic
Council, and Giuliano Castelli, a secretary who served Firmian. Their
aims were to secure the interests of the farmers and to impose a fierce
despotism on Lombardy by increasing Firmian's power and eliminating
the rights and pivileges of the Milanese patriciate. The plan, as revealed
in a series of conferences convened in Vienna during the spring and
summer of 1771, called for higher land taxes, the undermining of
reforms in indirect taxation, which would necessitate a continuation of
the Farm, the weakening of the Senate, the probable abolition of the
Congregation of State and Milan's Tribunal of Provision, and the
general degradation of the patricians, who were branded rebels and
refractories. Verri attended the conferences, opposed everything and
expected the worst: all civic agencies would disappear, all criticism
would end and the country would be plunged into slavery.(177)

> Firmian, dominated by Castelli and seconded by Lottinger, sees only
> enemies in the public bodies and the Senate . . . The greed and pride of
> the two obscure, ardent favorites poison his heart and push him to
> reduce the nobles to the last humiliation. The deception which has
> been used for so many years is to make it appear that the Milanese . . .
> are bad Austrians, secret rebels . . . and contraveners of every
> resolution emanating from the court. With this art the complaints of
> the public representatives are discredited and the person of the
> minister (Firmian) is always rendered more acceptable, as if he had the
> merit of holding in subjection a conquered people.

Verri was no neutral witness and his accusations, though having some
foundation, cannot be taken at face value.(178) But they do suggest the
passion and determination with which Carli and other crown officials
attempted to bear down on the Milanese aristocrats, whose
domestication was a major negative purpose of the Economic Council
and of the Censimento.

However the land tax was primarily a positive reform, concerned
more with the society at large than the politics of Milan, and its
managers spent most of their time receiving and following up reports
from the field. In this activity, which began right after the law's
enactment, the goal was modest liberty as well as strict compliance, a
clearer expression of the two-fold nature of enlightened absolutism in
Lombardy than the campaign against the patricians. From the summer
of 1761 until the end of 1765 the agency in charge of the tax was the
Cameral Magistracy, and though some of its members had abetted the
assessment revision scandal it seems to have worked honestly and in

conformity with the intentions of the second Giunta, perhaps because Governor Firmian did not trust it and maintained a careful watch over it.(179) In any event its first task was to deal with the fact that the country-side was quite generally violating, evading and twisting the new regulations. Faulty exactor contracts caused disputes, improper collection of taxes and occasionally the flight of collectors with the communal payment. Property deputies and collectors conspired to establish two personal rolls, a short one for Milan and a long (real) one for local use which produced a secret surplus; or the same officials let powerful owners keep their peasants off the personal list entirely. Elsewhere councils ignored statutory duties which they considered arduous and inconvenient: one village would have no *revisore* to audit the annual accounts, another would not hold the personal tax convocation nor expose the personal roll for scrutiny. Consequently even without malfeasance communal budgets were disorderly or in deficit, and individuals did not pay their fair share of taxes. A major source of abuse was the indifference of landlords toward the political institutions of the Censimento. Often the property convocations, essential for the discussion of communal finances and the selection of communal leaders, suffered paralysis from the lack of participation. Indeed in this respect the deputies were as bad as the constituents.

> The property deputies and their substitutes and the various owners are so careless about the general convocation . . . that meetings cannot open because not a single proprietor appears.

Yet the most alarming news came from convocations which were scenes of verbal and physical violence rather than quiescence, for the many public elections and assemblies had actually created an uproar on the land. An edict of March 1763, noting with dismay that in some general convocations men were "instigating tumults and insulting and vituperating property deputies," forbade under pain of immediate incarceration the formation of any group to oppose the observation of the census law or the execution of royal decrees.(180)

While the last order addressed "any person of whatever grade, status or condition," the specific steps which ministers took in the face of disturbances and offenses demonstrated that for them the great need was to curb the powers still wielded in communes by small owners and landless peasants. The apathy of owners, their low attendance at convocations and their tendency to reelect the same deputies again and again, evils in themselves, above all raised the specter that government in the country would fall back into the hands of the humble people who dwelt there and did not come just at certain times of the year to collect rents, perform political acts and get a breath of fresh air.

There is an evident danger that the administration of the public patrimony will become the arbitrary and despotic possession of a few owners. Since many deputies who live away from the area do not bother to appoint substitutes, those looking after daily affairs and always available for emergencies will control the commune.

Election practices such as voting with voices instead of secret ballots, the accumulation of many proxies by one person and the choosing of personal, commercial and property deputies at the same assembly; or the holding of property convocations in private homes and the failure to notify all proprietors of coming meetings: these irregularities too signified cabals and intrigues in favor of the poor and at the expense of the rich. In December of 1764 the Cameral Magistracy decided on corrective action, hoping to improve the "quality of persons" entering the office of property deputy. A series of commands affirmed the necessity of secret ballots, restricted the use of proxies and banned overt partisanship. A standard and rigorous method was introduced for summoning to convocation the absentee property deputies, their substitutes, "and also the principal owners." Property deputies were limited to one term, except when the new candidate was "litigatious and turbulent," and supported by a faction or party, in which case the election could be annulled and the incumbent retained. Finally the election of personal and commercial deputies must take place within their own convocations and away from the property meetings, "so as to avoid the confusions and tumults which can arise from mixing together simple *personalisti* and owners."(181) In short the men who succeeded Neri, despite many frustrations, never lost his faith that "the legitimate representation and true voice of the respective communities reside precisely in the general convocation," and that the property deputies exercised a "legitimate procuration" for the commune.(182)

Carli composed the above phrases in June of 1780 on the eve of his retirement, appropriately imitating in language and emphasis the opening page of the communal law of 1755. Indeed in the past thirty years policy toward the land had been broadly uniform and unchanging, and by now the operation of the Censimento was a matter of routine. Royal officials continued to complain of lapses and errors, collusion between property deputies and exactors being still common in 1785, but as Carli also wrote in 1780, "the architecture of the system detects disorders, natural enough in the country-side, so much more easily as the harmony of its parts is more perfect."(183) Surprisingly the president of the Economic Council was not himself in complete agreement with this smooth course and in various ways attempted to deflect or contain the liberal thrust which the Neri years had lent the reform movement. Given his business ventures in Istria, the honored station which he reserved for gentlemen in his literary works, and especially his trenchant praise of the land tax for encouraging agriculture, he ought to have been a champion of rural development and of those who advanced it. Certainly one side of him was so inclined, as he again evinced in 1771 when he criticized Verri's *Meditazione sull' economia politica* because it favored small holdings and forgot that owners of large estates improved the soil and increased productivity. He was just as negative about the author's plan to curtail peasant unemployment and the harm of excessive irrigation by indirectly hindering rice and dairy farming, noting instead that such enterprises used the land well, brought in ample revenue and quickly compensated the nation for any incidental losses.(184) Yet at bottom Carli was neither an economic nor a political liberal, and he did not believe that the state should impel men, not even elites, to pursue their interests wholeheartedly. While his published essay on the Censimento (1784) described in detail the communal and provincial reforms, granted the "maxim" that public administration must include persons who were "interested," the proprietors, and applauded their coming together in a "species of parliament," his secret essay of 1768, generally more candid and representative of his views, never mentioned the councils and assemblies; and in his confidential correspondence with Kaunitz he remarked that his principal task was to hold local leaders in subordination and force them to supply exact financial statements.(185) He was equally stern in formulating a position on the marketing of grain, an issue which came before the Economic Council after 1767. He and a majority of the councilors opposed significant loosening of the current regulations, judging that a landlocked country like Lombardy, surrounded by hungry neighbors, was peculiarly susceptible to scarcity, but he alone stressed the inherently anti-social temper of big landlords. In December of 1766 he told Firmian that the "greed of owners" was always a problem for ministers dealing with famine conditions, and two years later his report of the Council decision to retain controls explained that since barely five percent of the Lombard population possessed exportable surpluses, the crown could not possibly make everyone else dependent upon a few magnates, "who have no other cares than their own regardless of the common good." In the midst of the debate he did not hesitate to turn upside-down the meaning of the Censimento: the assistance which landlords got from it was not an argument for bestowing on them fresh freedoms; rather because of it they required no further stimulation.(186) At the same time he advised Vienna that

public and guild supervision of urban business was an essential means of
preventing "disorder, bad faith and inertia."(187)

> In proportion as nations have abandoned liberty in manufacturing and
> commerce and imposed discipline, the arts have progressed and riches
> multiplied.

Moreover if in reality Carli was the guardian of a society which he hoped
would prosper, in fantasy his ideal became a place where economic
activity hardly existed. His *Delle lettere americane,* written in the late
1770's, venerated Sparta and Peru for preferring moral superiority over
material achievement. The Inca princes, he claimed, had discovered the
secret of perfect government which was to ban all private surplus and
confiscate property whenever the owner exceeded the needs of subsistence. Already in *L'Uomo libero* he had hinted obscurely that peoples
might shorten or avoid their painful journey to monarchy through the
ruins of civil war by learning the lessons of Peruvian history.(188)

In the daily administration of Lombardy there was nothing foolish or
reprehensible about Carli's conservatism. The fear which he shared with
Kaunitz concerning high food prices in Milan was vindicated by the
example of Tuscany where urban bread riots in 1790 broke the reform
party and swept away the liberal grain laws.(189) His feeling that the
monarchy was vulnerable in the city because the patricians could easily
fan and minipulate popular discontent must have strengthened his
conviction that agriculture should not be specially invited to open new
markets and charge more for its products. He was also more acute than
many of his critics in realizing that peasants bought grain as often as
they sold it and therefore would not benefit automatically from free
trade.(190) On the question of regulating commerce and manufacturing
his fulminations against "undefined liberty" reflected his general state
of mind, not his specific plans, which in fact envisioned the preservation
of only a few guilds and defended the right of individuals to set up shop
anywhere they wished without harassment provided they obeyed the
civil laws.(191) Nonetheless perhaps it is true, as Franco Venturi
suggests, that in the large perspective, in an age of transformation and a
country escaping from generations of stagnation, Carli was too cautious
and empirical.(192) The work of beginning anew, of fashioning the
Western Enlightenement, demanded the optimism and boldness of a
man like Verri while in his heart of hearts Carli was a pessimist. His
close and technical critique of Verri's book contained the bleak universal
remark that nature left to herself

> is wild and unformed, destructive as much as productive, proceeding
> with death, sickness and depredation toward ends which we cannot
> fathom.

He then added that man, usually misconstruing his interests, would not surmount his ignorance and indolence unless authority and violence dragged him on.(193) The Austrians at least preferred that he control this penchant for gloom and keep the balance in his personality between traditional and modern elements, the combination which probably had attracted them in the first place, and which enabled him to promote and protect the machinery of reform by defying rigid adherents of the old society and accomodating those who could accept and serve the new. Gently but firmly they instructed him to follow what one might call the true logic of the Censimento, and so in the end his exceptions only proved the rule.

In June of 1770 Kaunitz told Carli that Verri's idea of abolishing all the guilds was not, as he had charged, a prescription for anarchy and barbarism, and that he, Carli, should try to reach common ground with his colleague, since after all everyone must agree on the need for a ''discreet regime'' which would subject the arts and manufacturing as little as possible to restriction and intervention.(194) A few years later Vienna urged its officials in Milan to expose the ''futility and inconvenience'' of laws which compelled the country-side to announce the grain harvest and introduce much of it into the cities, ''laws which offend the authority of the legislator when not observed, and when observed offend a major part of the population, the proprietors and the peasants.'' In 1781 Emperor Joseph found that every unnecessary limitation on the internal and external circulation of grain was ''contrary to the progress and prosperity of agriculture, the most constant and secure source of national riches.''(195) Meanwhile another dispute had arisen between Carli and his superiors over a matter which involved the Censimento with particular immediacy — the disposition of common lands.(196) The reform act of 1755 sanctioned the ''promiscuous use'' of communal property and assigned the personal deputy the task of insuring that large owners did not interfere with a right so essential for his constituents. Through the next decade government policy remained friendly toward the commons, perhaps because their occasional misappropriation produced some of the unrest which was disturbing the rural assemblies. In November of 1763, eight months after calling for calm in the communes, the Cameral Magistracy conveyed Maria Theresa's ''sovereign irrevocable will'' to guard the commons on behalf of the poor, and ordered property deputies and chancellors, under threat of fine, to get back any such land given up since 1760, even if they must borrow the required money.(197) Carli, though an innovator and a fairly harsh master on his own estates in Istria, approved Vienna's stance, warning in 1776 that economic theory should never be confused with the reality of the Lombard country-side where peasants deprived of the commons simply would flee.(198) However the key ministers now thought differently and in June of 1779 they decreed a general alienation of the commons, even allowing solvent buyers to acquire property from debt-free communes by paying 3½ percent annual interest and no principal at all. Here is their imperial preamble.

> With the various provident measures emanating from Our Throne . . . in favor of agriculture in our State of Milan — the proportionate and uniform taxation of land and individuals through the Censimento, the free internal circulation of grain and the facile exportation of surpluses — Our aim was to encourage the industry of the cultivator and augment the nation's riches. In the main success has corresponded with our expectations. But because communities cannot fructify moors and sterile or watery areas which they hold in common there is still much waste land. Hence we believe that in the interests of the larger public and of the communes themselves the uncultivated common lands should pass into the hands of private owners prepared to improve them.

This statement deserves to stand beside Carli's explanation of fixed assessments as providing deep insight into the nature and purpose of the great tax reform.

Actually the use of the commons was an issue only in the hills and dry plains since on the irrigated plains they had practically disappeared long before, and in the mountains they were so extensive, 71 percent of the measured land, and so woven into the fabric of life, that few contemplated changing their status, which the edict of 1779 specifically did not affect. But an ugly conflict took place in the first two regions where during the century following the survey communal property fell from 11 to .5 percent of the valued whole.(199) One riven community, Cardano, near the town of Varese, has been studied, and its experience gives an idea of what the process of enclosure was like. Until 1779 the fight centered on the interpretation of traditional arrangements, supposedly frozen by the Censimento, with the little people insisting that most of the common land was open to them for grazing and gathering wood and dung. The clamor was sufficiently loud for the sound of it to reach Milan repeatedly between 1766 and 1778, and in the latter year some of the wealthy owners asked the tax office to impose on the peasants *(personalisti)* exemplary punishments as a way of repressing their arrogance, and to bar those with low assessments from the property convocation. Certainly the rustics were at a disadvantage in hotly advocating free commons, whatever the legal merits of their case, because the system of local government established in the 1750s cast them and their leaders in the role of humble petitioners who always behaved with patience and resignation. Indeed the judgment which the Economic Council rendered in April of 1771 lacked all sympathy for them despite the fact that Carli fully understood how important the waste land was for their subsistence and minimum comfort.

> The personal deputy of Cardano pretends that his people before the census had two thirds of the communal moors and the owners one third. The property deputies refute the claim in a brief which shows that their arguments are well founded. The tribunal of the Censimento has decided three times that the moors belong to the owners, and we confirm and persist in the decision. To end the inquietude of the petitioners we make . . . formal notification to Antonio Ferazzo (personal deputy) and Giuseppe Aspese, the principal complainants, that they must accept our directive or be imprisoned.

When the edict of 1779 transformed the terms of the debate, the response of the Cardano peasants was to demand that communal property be sold in small, cheap lots which they could afford. Already in September of 1779 the crown had ordered officials and representatives to sell just peripheral commons in large blocks while dividing those near the village and reserving them in first choice for residents.(200) Nonetheless in 1780 and 1781 two or three rich buyers obtained over half of Cardano's moors and woods, 113 out of 200 hectares, and in January of 1782 the crowd interrupted an auction with shouts that the lots being offered were still too big. The next month even the first deputy, no doubt under pressure from medium owners as well as the very poor, joined with the other deputies in seeking permission from Milan to make the sales more convenient for small buyers in the community. Yet no one dared protest the rule that the successful aspirant for every plot, large or small, near or far, must have promised to cultivate it more quickly than his rivals.(201) On the contrary, a rich Cardano owner named Tranquillo Mari cautioned the Tribunal that several peasants schemed to buy land for the purpose of keeping it waste. Not surprisingly the same Tranquillo Mari convinced Milan in 1794 that it should not now ask for the cash payments which creditable purchasers like himself had been holding back for many years. Thus the large proprietors enjoyed royal favor in the division of public land, learning from the enclosure movement how the new political and administrative institutions would give them their way in the country-side so long as they pursued modern economic and social goals instead of subverting the tax law.

CONCLUSION

The Censimento undoubtedly made the imposition of direct taxes in Lombardy more equitable, regular and honest than it had been in the past. If those most privileged under the old system did not appreciate the change, for other landowners the benefits were real and should have been gratifying. Nonetheless the overall impact of the reform, with its many indirect and intangible effects, is difficult to gage. Through it the country lost autonomy and became increasingly dependent upon the good will and decency of the Austrians, whose policies, concerned with a far greater range of affairs than simply the welfare of their Italian subjects, might at any moment degenerate into harsh exploitation or destructive whim. In fact Vienna acted with considerable restraint, at least until the reign of Joseph, but the uneasiness of a progressive official like Pietro Verri at the possibility of tyrannical rule in Lombardy explains why opposition to the work of Miro and Neri, however much influenced by selfish interests, was always attractive and persuasive. On the other hand the usual defenses against a great power such as Austria (or Spain) were obstruction and obfuscation, debilitating tactics which, even when successful, isolated the land spiritually and hindered the resolution of domestic problems. Hence some natives could find in the rationalization and integration brought by the cadaster a true sense of joy and fulfillment. The reading of Neri's *Progress Report* was a fundamental and formative experience for the young Verri(202), and perhaps the Cremonese orator Giambattista Freganeschi, while an older man, reacted similarly. Indeed the joint reply of 1758 which Freganeschi helped to prepare on behalf of Cremona, Lodi, Pavia and Casal Maggiore suggests that a minority of Lombard leaders supported and valued the slow transformation of their homeland into a more cohesive polity, and accepted a larger role for the dynasty as necessary or appropriate.

Moreover, besides being a splended instrument of monarchical administration the tax initiated important economic, political and social programs. The probity and certainty with which fiscal burdens were assigned and exacted, and especially the stability of assessments, stimulated agriculture after 1760, and farm property became more valuable and profitable for owners. Within the limits of a flawed technology proprietors siezed the opportunity thus presented, though probably they were not immediately as grateful for it as Vincenzo Dandolo was a half century later. At the same time they received from the crown a share in local government which if nothing else intensified their control over the peasantry by letting them limit the area of commons and diminish the authority of able rustics who traditionally held village office and manipulated village finances. Admittedly the *estimati* did not obtain political rights and social status which fully compensated some of them for the deprivation of old fashioned liberty and esteem, or which could give them the enviable situation enjoyed by citizens in the pre-democratic constitutional regimes of the 19th century. The conversion of nobles into notables, insofar as it actually took place, was no cataclysm in a country where feudal titles and prerogatives were relatively insignificant and middling groups posed little threat to the established hierarchy. Neither was it a spontaneous and voluntary process, for those undergoing it had no guarantee that the advantages would be substantial and permanent. The assemblies and councils of the Censimento, in other words, were not designed as institutions which could formally challenge and check the executive. On the contrary the demise of so many personal and corporate privileges made the Austrians much stronger in Lombardy after 1760 than before. Yet in an imprecise way the notables also became civil nobles, secure in their grip on the land, familiar with the central piece of legislation regulating their lives, and in possession of the means for constantly asking assistance of a government which afterall wanted their friendship and comfort. The imperial reformers, fighting hard against Milanese patricians and their like in order to dominate a province which had been gained in war, channeled their new power through laws that set high standards of administrative conduct, and used their additional leverage to favor landowners over peasants. The result was a workable blend of despotism and liberality which elites could tolerate and which historians might well designate with the ambiguous compound phrase enlightened absolutism.

NOTES

(1) *The Wealth of Nations* (Homewood, Ill., 1963), 2: 329-30. Smith also conveyed some misinformation about the tax.

(2) Gianrinaldo Carli, letter to Pompeo Neri (1771), in *Scrittori classici italiani di economia politica, Parte moderna*, ed., P. Custodi (Milan, 1804), 14: 381; *idem*, ''Relazione del Censimento dello Stato di Milano (1784),'' in *Scrittori classici, Parte moderna*, 14: 291.

(3) *La Riforma finanziaria nella Lombardia austriaca nel XVIII secolo*, ed. C.A. Vianello (Milan, 1940), 451, 461.

(4) Carlo Cattaneo, *Scritti economici*, ed. A. Bertolino (Florence, 1956), 3: 279-80; *idem, Scritti storici e geografici*, ed. G. Salvemini & E. Sestan (Florence, 1957), 1: 416-18; *idem, Scritti politici*, ed. M. Boneschi (Florence, 1965), 4: 414-23.

(5) Guiseppe Ricca-Salerno, *Storia delle doctrine finanziarie in Italia* (Palermo, 1896), 216. Currently: *Storia di Milano* (Milan, 1959), 12: 136-7, 255, 284, 490, 503: Franco Catalano, *Illuministi e giacobini del settecento italiano* (Milan-Varese, 1959), 77-8; Giorgio Candeloro, *Storia dell'Italia moderna* (Milan, 1956), 1; 85; Franco Venturi, *Settecento riformatore* (Turin, 1969), 432, 436-7; Salvatore Pugliese, ''Condizione economiche e finanziarie della Lombardia nella prima metà del secolo XVIII,'' in *Miscellanea di storia italiana* (Turin, 1924), 489-90.

(6) Rosario Romeo argues that the relative health of Italian agriculture and the unequal distribution of agricultural profits were of fundamental importance in creating an industrial base for the country after unification: *Risorgimento e capitalismo* (Bari, 1963), 111-64, 197-203. Even Romeo's critics agree that the large scale agriculture of North Italy played a significant role in 19th century economic development. See Alexander Gerschenkron, *Continuity in History and other Essays* (Cambridge, Mass., 1968), 108-09; *idem, Economic Backwardness in Historical Perspective* (Cambridge, Mass., 1962), 96, 106-18; Dario Tosi, ''Sulle forme iniziali di sviluppo economico e i loro effetti nel lungo periodo: l'agricultura italiana e l'accumulazione capitalistica,'' in *Annali dell'Istitutov Giangiacomo Feltrinelli*, 4 (1961), 199-223. New support for Romeo is in Valerio Castronovo, *Economia e società in Piemonte dall'unità al 1914* (Milan, 1969): see the review in *American Historical Review*, 75 (1970), 2093-4. The effect of the Censimento on Lombard agriculture is discussed below.

(7) For general works see note 5 above; also Franco Valsecchi, *L'assolutismo illuminato in Austria e in Lombardia* (Bologna, 1934), 2: 1-112. Partial studies are: Carlo Lupi, *Storia de' principi, delle massime e regole seguite nelle formazione del catasto prediale introdotto nello stato di Milano l'anno 1760* (Milan, 1825); Sergio Zaninelli, *Il nuovo censo dello stato di Milano dall'editto del 1718 al 1733* (Milan, 1963); *idem*, ''Un 'Progretto d'un nuovo sistema di Taglia da pratticarsi nello stato di Milano' del 1709,'' *Archivio storico lombardo*, ser 8, vol 10 (1960), 535-86; Bruno Caizzi, *Il Comasco sotto il dominio austriaco fino alla redazione del catasto teresiano* (Como, 1955);

Catalano, *Il luministi*, 77-105. Zaninelli, *Il nuovo censo*, 11, promises a second volume on the period to 1760; Venturi, *Settecento*, 435, refers to a full scale study in progress by Marino Beregno. I have not seen Cotta Morandini, *Il censimento milanese* (Milan, 1832), 3 vols.

(8) The *Progress Report* (hereafter *PR)* is: Pompeo Neri, *Relazione dello stato in cui si trova l'opera del Censimento universale del Ducato di Milano nel mese di maggio dell'anno 1750*(Milan, 1750). Supposedly Neri was in contact with French officials in the late 1750's and prepared for them a ''Progetto d'un sistema censuario per la Francia.'' Lupi, *Storia*, 152-4; Gaetano Rocchi, ''Pompeo Neri,'' *Archivio storico italiano*, 24 (1876), 260, 450. According to the representative of France at Florence in 1765, the French controller-general Bertin had a copy of the *PR*. Corrado Vivanti, *Le campagne del Mantovano nell'età delle riforme*(Milan, 1959), 109-11. In 1767 Alessandro Verri, then in Paris, gave the book to Andre Morellet. *Carteggio di Pietro e di Alessandro Verri*, ed. E. Greppi (Milan, 1923), 1 (Part 1): 283. François Véron de Forbonnois, ''Précis historique du cadastre établi dans le duchè de Milan,'' in *Principes et observations oeconomiques*(Amsterdam, 1767), 2: 243-84; Jean Louis Moreau de Beaumont, *Mémoires concernant les impositions et droits en Europe et en France*(Paris, 1768), 1: 264-85. Lupi, *Storia*, 153-4, states that during the occupation of Lombardy the French carefully examined the Censimento with the explicit intention of using it as a model for France. The ar-chitect of the Napoleonic census, Martin-Michel Gaudin (Duc de Gaete), recalled after 1815 that he and his countrymen had been encouraged by their own traditions and by the example of neighboring states such as ''the Milanese.'' ''Mémoire sur le cadastre,'' in *Mémoires* (Paris, 1834), 3 (*Supplément*): 203.

(9) Marcel Marion, *Les impôts directs sous l'ancien régime* (Paris, 1910), 65-9, 102-09, 297-302; idem, *Histoire financière de la France depuis 1715* (Paris, 1914), 1: 171-5, 184-6, 196-225; voll 4 (1925): 256, 309-12; Rene Stourm, *Les finances de l'ancien régime et de la révolution* (Paris, 1885), 1: 55, 62-5, 88-91, 136-41, 192-4; Georges Weulersse, *Le mouvement physiocratique en France*(Paris, 1910), 1: 468-73; Gaudin, ''Mémoire sur le cadastre,'' 201-87.

(10) Louis Philippe May, ''Despotisme légal et despotisme éclairé d'après Le Mercier de la Rivière,'' *Bulletin of the International Committee of Historical Sciences*, 9 (No. 34, 1937), 62-3; Michel Lhèritier, ''Rapport génerál: Le despotisme éclairé de Frederic II à la révolution française,'' *Bulletin*, 9 (No. 35, 1937), 209: also Thadd E. Hall, ''Thought and Practice of Enlightened Government in French Corsica,'' *American Historical Review*, 74 (1969), 894.

(11) Valsecchi in *Storia di Milano*, 12: 284 (also 255, 277-8); idem, *L'assolutismo*, 2: 64-6; Mario Romani in *Storia di Milano*, 12: 490 499, 502; Pugliese, ''Condizione economiche,'' 126, 456.

(12) Valsecchi in *Storia di Milano*, 12: 354-5; the remark was first made in 1934 in *L'assolutismo*, 2: 198. Also stressing bourgeois interests and aspirations are: Catalano, *Illuministi*, 77, 259 (''The actions (of enlightened sovereigns) had worked to the advantage of the bourgeoisie, though they had not been precisely conscious of favoring any particular class, but had only searched for allies in their fights with the nobility and the church.''); idem, ''Il probleme delle affitanze nella seconda meta del settecento in un' inchiesta piemontese del

1793," *Annali dell'Istituto Giangiacomo Feltrinelli,* 2 (1959) 429-34; Candeloro, *Storia,* 1:83; and as a tentative suggestion, Pugliese, "Condizione economiche," 454-5.

Already in 1911 Ettore Rota had called Verri the "thermometer of bourgeois opinion," *L'Austria in Lombardia e la preparazione del movimento democratico cisalpino* (Rome-Milan-Naples, 1911), 34. Cautioning against this kind of analysis are Franco Venturi, *Utopia and Reform in the Enlightenment* (Cambridge, 1971), 10-12; Mario Romani in *Storia di Milano,* 12: 523.

(13) See Valsecchi's fine sketch of the political reforms in *L'assolutismo,* 2: 89-98.

(14) Several of the topics in this paragraph are discussed below in more detail. The best population estimates indicate 900,000+ in 1750 and between 1 and 1.1 million in 1770: Gianrinaldo Carli, "Saggio di economia pubblica (1768)," in *Saggi inediti di G.R. Carli,* ed. C. A. Vianello (Florence, 1938), 79-80; C.A. Vianello, *Il settecento milanese* (Milan, 1934), 218, 279-80; Pugliese, "Condizione economiche," 60-1; Pietro Verri, "Sulle leggi vincolanti principalmente nel commercio de' grani (1769)," in *Scrittori classici, Parte moderna,* 16: 144-6; also the criticism by Verri of Carli's figures in *La riforma finanzaria,* 31-2. On the size of Lombardy and the 18th century dismemberments, Pugliese, "Condizione economiche," 16-25; Mario Romani, *L'agricoltura in Lombardia dal periodo delle riforme al 1859* (Milan, 1957), 19-21.

(15) Pugliese, "Condizione echonomiche," 16-25; Bruno Caizzi, *Industria, commercio e banca in Lombardia nel XVIII secolo* (Milan, 1968), 44-5; Romani, *L'agricoltura,* 11-15, 29-34, 163-71.

(16) Pugliese, acknowledged master of the Censimento records, supplied figures on land ownership which all later historians accepted: "Condizione economiche," 71-8, 455, 459; Romani, *L'agricoltura,* 59-76. Unfortunately none of the authors explain clearly what they mean by nobility, noble class, privileged land, etc. Valsecchi, *L'Italia nel seicento e nel settecento* (Turin, 1967), 164, attributes Pugliese's four ninths exclusively to the 300 patrician families of Milan, whose numbers he then places at "a little more than one percent of the population," an impossible calculation. Vianello, *Il settecento,* 61, 66, 285-9, agreeing that one percent, the nobles, owned four ninths, establishes that the noble population of Milan, patricians and others, was 5,160, about .5 percent of the total. He also notes that of the 39 persons in Lombardy in 1750 owning more than 10,000 Milanese *pertiche* of land, 31 had Milanese patrician names and combine holdings of 757,000 *pertiche,* a large sum but still only 16 percent of the four ninths. The best discussions of the Lombard nobility are by Gulio Vismara and Bruno Caizzi in *Storia di Milano,* 11: 225-82, 335-53. The former states: "It is much easier to list the Milan patrician families, even in their vicissitudes, than to define their status or ascertain their historic relationship with the nobility, from which they sprang and replenished their numbers." To join the Milanese patriciate, a formal class, families had to show that they had lived nobly in the city or its countryside for over 100 years. Generally all city dwelling landowners, including a few business men, could be considered *nobili,* through there were also rural nobles. Between 1706 and 1780 Charles VI and Maria Theresa granted to individuals 233 Lombard titles and feudatories, of which 48 went to Milanese patricians, 178 to "altri nobili dello stato" and the rest to foreigners (*Storia di Milano,* 12: xi). For

the relative unimportance of Lombard feudalism, Romani, *L'agricoltura,* 47-53; Pugliese, "Condizione economiche," 139-40.

Romani, 93-105, discusses the paradoxical situation of the plains leaseholders, whom landlords treated as minor partners despite the fact that they were the great entrepreneurs of Lombard agriculture and the most distinguished men having continuous contact with the peasantry. See also Cattaneo, *Scritti economici,* 3: 134-5. On tax farmers, Pugliese, "Condizione econmiche," 179-80, 194.

(17) On the Spanish tax, *PR,* 1-86, 109-26, 249-68 (including the Commission reports of 1733); the quote, 36-7. Neri's description has the support of Bruno Caizzi, *Il Comasco sotto il dominio spagnolo* (Como, 1955), chap. 1 & 2; *idem, Il Comasco sotto il dominio austriaco* (Como, 1955), 79; and Pugliese, "Condizione economiche," 263-9, 293-309, 474-89: ". . . the monstrosity of the Spanish fiscal system supplies the reason for the rapid and grave decadence suffered by Lombardy, which related more to this cause than to wars, famines and plagues."

(18) On the *Diaria,* Pugliese, "Condizione economiche,", 269-80. Comparison with the *Mensulae,* which averaged about 7.4 million *lira* per year between 1701 and 1706, is approximate, both taxes involving many extra charges. Zaninelli, "Un Progetto," 539, 547, emphasizes that the *Diaria* was itself an important reform which unified most military costs under one heading and transferred control of expenditure from local to royal officials. In 1721 after the fighting ended the *Diaria* fell to 13,000 *lira* per day; in 1713 it was 3 million *lira* in arrears. The Lombard *lira* was not a coin or bill but an imaginary money or money of account, worth in 1750 about 3.5 grams of fine silver and equal to 1/33 of an English pound: Caizzi, *Industria,* i; Verri, "Sulle leggi," 251. According to Pugliese (p. 12), the *lira* depreciated 6 % between 1700 and 1750.

(19) On Prass and his pamphlet, Zaninelli, "Un progetto," *passim* (an appendix contains the complete text). Prass' identity is uncertain but apparently he lived in Brussles and was perhaps Piedmontese by birth. Another copy of the pamphlet and replies from the city of Milan, the province of Pavia, the province of Tortona, the city and province of Vigevano, the town of Voghera, the city and province of Cremona, and the *Giunta di Governo,* the committee which ruled Lombardy in Eugene's absence, are in *Miscellanea: Censo ed imposte* (number 3), a bound, unpaginated volume in the Biblioteca Nazionale Braidenese of Milan. Zaninelli, who has made a careful study of unpublished material, also discusses the replies of Casal Maggiore, the province of Milan, the city and province of Lodi, the city of Pavia, and the Congregation of State.

(20) Already in 1712 the *Giunta di Governo* told Vienna that the provinces were asking for a land survey. The best example of this royal interpretation, the source of the quoted phrases, is the proclamation of 14 April 1719 ordering proprietors to supply information about their holdings; also the letter of the Miro Commission to the Congregation of State of 11 May 1719; and the Commission order of 27 June 1726 concerning the personal tax. These documents are in the appendix of Zaninelli, *Il nuovo censo,* 113-4, 139. Also the royal edict of 1749 establishing the Neri Commission recalled the appeals of forty years earlier: *Raccolta degli editti, ordini, istruzione, riforme e lettere circolare istrutive della Real Giunta del Censimento Generale dello Stato di Milano,* 2d ed. (Milan, 1802), part 1: 3. Hereafter *Raccolta Giunta.*

(21) *Histoire financière,* 1: 208-09.

(21a) For this paragraph see Zaninelli, "Un progetto," 557; *idem, Il nuovo censo,* 21-4, 30, 87-8.

(22) Zaninelli, *Il nuovo censo, passim; PR,* 95-102.

(23) *PR,* 349-50, 357-8.

(24) Carli, "Relazione del Censimento," 270; *Raccolta degli editti, ordini, istruzioni e lettere circolari pubblicati dalla Regia Provisionale Delegazione del Censimento generale dello Stato di Milano,* 2d ed. (Milan, 1802), 3-4, 16, 26-38. Hereafter *Raccolta Provisionale Delegazione.* Lucia Sebastiani, *La tassazione degli ecclesiastici nella Lombardia teresiana* (Milan-Rome, 1969), 9, 18. Legitimate secular exemptions were "onerous" (*onerosa*), obtained by purchase or some other acceptable means rather than through usurpation (*esenzioni abusive o gratuiti*). They were valid for royal and provincial taxes but not communal charges. In general the agents of the Censimento made only oblique references to onerous exemptions and never discussed them in detail. An example is the order of 29 February 1772 concerning the taxation of previously exempt church lands: "If by chance the registry of immune church property also includes laic lands holding onerous exemptions disregard these last as they have nothing to do with the present tax." *Raccolta degli editti, ordini, istruzione e lettere circolare pubblicati dal Magistrato Camerale e successivi governi* (Milan, 1802), 34. Hereafter *Raccolta Magistrato Camerale.* Here and elsewhere I leave out of account the exemptions for families with twelve children, which, valid for personal as well as land taxes, was not considered a privilege and apparently gave relief mainly to the poor. See *Raccolta Provisionale Delegazione,* 60. The *scudo* equalled six *lira.*

(24a) "We propose to relate the distribution of taxes in 1599 to the present value of the state and the number of taxable individuals recorded by the census of 1730, establishing the amount which each *scudo* and each individual may withold from each tax . . . With the separate division of each tax, the value of each exemption, set according to the royal edict of 20 February 1732, will be placed in the cadastral book beside the property to which it belongs." Zaninelli, *Il nuovo censo,* 157, 167. However in the end because of insufficient documentation the Giunta simply assumed that direct taxes had tripled since the 16th century and so prepared to reduce by one third any charge on which someone held an acceptable exemption. *Storia di Milano,* 12: 138.

(25) In addition to Zaninelli, *Il nuovo censo,* see the *PR,* 281-96, which contains another version of the unified tax plan with a covering letter.

(26) The Giunta dedicated a special memorandum to the separations in March of 1733, published in full in the *PR,* 109-26. The quote, 119. Feudal and non-feudal communes were not joined, nor two feudal communes unless under the same lord.

(27) Valsecchi, *L'assolutismo,* 2: 64-8.

(28) Luigi Dal Pane, *La finanza toscana dagli inizi del secolo XVIII alla caduta del Granducato* (Milan, 1965), 119-37; Herman Büchi, *Finanzpolitik Toskanas im Zeitalter der Aufklarung* (Berlin, 1915), chap. 5; Furio Diaz, *Francesco Maria Gianni* (Milan-Naples, 1966), chap. 4.

(29) See note 20 above; also Neri, *PR,* viii-ix, 90; Carli, "Relazione del Censimento," 237. The remarks of Neri, Carli and the government were taken at face value by Moreau de Beaumont, *Mémoires concernant les impositions,* 1: 280-1; and (in the 19th century) Lupi, *Storia de 'principi,* 30-1.

(30) *PR*, xi-xv, xvii, 32.

(31) *La riforma finanzaria*, 461.

(31) Zaninelli, *Il nuovo censo*, 17-18, is emphatic that no comprehensive understanding of the *Mensuale* and the *Diaria* existed outside the government in the first part of the century.

(33) See note 19 above. The Pavians drew inspiration from Vauban (*Dixme royale*) and Boisguilbert (the "unknown author" of the *Testament politique du maréchal de Vauban*), mentioning their writings as if they were well known in Lombardy. They considered, not too deeply, the commercial nature of agriculture and the function of money and investment in maintaining the level of domestic economic activity. Hence Zaninelli, *Il nuovo censo*, 17-18, may be too quick in assuming the lack of "economic consciousness" before 1750.

(34) On the depression, Romani, *Storia di Milano*, 12: 482-5, 491-6; Pugliese, "Condizione economiche," 92-104, 196; Caizzi, *Industria*, 44.

(35) On the bank and the ability of nobles to accomodate themselves, Romani, *Storia di Milano*, 12: 486-8, 499; on moneylenders, 45-6, 49-50 below.

(36) *PR*, xii, 156-61 (examples of criticism of the Congregation); 173-4 (Miro's letter). For a different use of the *PR* see Romani, *Storia di Milano*, 12: 503-06; Rocchi, "Pompeo Neri," 256; Oscar Nuccio, biographic appendix in Neri, "Documenti annessi alle *Osservazione sopra il prezzo legale delle monete*," *Scrittori classici, Parte antica* (1814-1816; reprint ed., Rome, 1965), 7: xxviii.

(37) The "secret enemies" appear on many pages of the *PR*, e.g., xii; on 371 Neri warned the Congregation to beware of them; for local administrators, x and especially 72-86; on 315-16 Neri is very bitter toward Milan and its leaders.

(38) Zaninelli, *Il nuovo censo*, 29-30, 40-8; Neri, *PR*, 108.

(39) Marion, *Histoire financière*, 1: 181-6, 205-11; Weulersse, *Le mouvement psysiocratique*, 1: 468-73; Turgot, *Oeuvres*, ed. G. Schelle (Paris, 1914), 2: 290.

(40) Renato Zangheri, *La proprietà terriera e le origini del risorgimento nel Bolognese* (Bologna, 1961), chap. 2.

(41) For this paragraph see Zaninelli, *Il nuovo censo*, 49-66, 71-2, 75-82, 89-92; Lupi, *Storia de'principi*, 43-119; Neri, *PR*, 14, 127-52; Pugliese, "Condizione economiche," 53. The Milanese brief and two relevant petitions from the Congregation of State are in *Miscellanea: Censo ed imposte* (3) cited note 19 above. One of the petitions is dated 10 October 1726 and the other two compositions are from the same period.

(42) Zaninelli, *Il nuovo censo*, 77-8, 81-2, 85; Valsecchi, *L'assolutismo*, 2: 65.

(43) *PR*, 127-8.

(44) Congregation petition of 10 October (note 41 above).

(45) Zaninelli, *Una grande azienda agricola della pianura irrigua lombardia nei secoli XVIII e XIX* (Milan, 1964), 156-63.

(46) Zaninelli, *Il nuovo censo*, 77.

(47) The report is published in full by Neri, *PR*, 132-52; the quote, 146. Neri was as unhappy as Miro about the use of outsiders but he termed the 1732 evaluation "as good as humanly possible." (*PR*, 14, 128-9). See also Zaninelli, *Il nuovo censo*, 81-2, 89-91. Rice cultivation is discussed by Pugliese,

"Condizione economiche," 34-8; the hill contracts by Romani, *L'agricoltura*, 85-93.

(48) Lupi, *Storia de 'principi*, 69-70, 77-81, 100; the quote, 81.

(49) Neri, *PR*, 153-72; Zaninelli, *Il nuovo censo*, 63-6; Pugliese, "Condizione economiche," 53; Caizzi, *Industria*, 94. Also "Le piante de Moroni e d'altri fruitti considerate nel soggetto del Generale Censimento ovvero Discorso practico-legale nella questione (n.p., n.d., no pagination, probably 1726);" and "Dissertazione del Marchese Freganeschi Oratore della Città di Cremona per dimonstrare che nel nuovo generale Censimento i more-gelsi debono ser compresi nel censo (n.p., n.d., no pagination, probably 1753)," in *Miscellanea: Censo ed imposte* (number 1), a bound, unpaginated volume in the Biblioteca Nazionale Braidense of Milan. Only plants producing an annual harvest of 25 Milanese pounds (kg. 19.5) were counted, the worth of each being set at 5 *lira* capital value. The Giunta, Neri and Freganeschi argued that this was a moderate cost for owners while Milan described it as excessive. Pugliese believed that the mulberry plants were quite undervalued.

(50) "Le piante de Moroni."

(51) *PR*, 157-8 (Neri), 175 (Miro). Still in 1750 Neri apparently had no special plan for local government, noting only that new instructions would be required for the Congregation of State and for provincial and communal officers (*PR*, 361). In the Giunta report of 1732 on the separations there was also an inconclusive discussion of how the newly united communes might be administered (*PR*, 123-6; Zaninelli, *Il nuovo censo*, 102).

(52) Excerpts from the October report and the Miro letter are in Neri, *PR*, 162-75; the quote, 167.

(53) Serious opposition to reforming the *mercimonio* came only from Milan and Como, which wanted either no tax at all or one entirely administered and calculated by local officials. Nonetheless, to avoid delay and controversy, the Giunta decided, with the permission of the crown, to set the tax at an arbitrary figure, based on what had been paid in the period 1728-30, instead of surveying the commercial sector of the economy. Neri, *PR*, 188-205.

(54) "Relazione di ciò che ha pensato la Giunta sopra il censimento dei coloni (1757)," in Sebastiani, *La tassazione degli ecclesiastici*, 49-51. The royal edict of December 1755 stated: "(The personal tax) can never be increased even when there is a rise in the needs of the crown, provinces or communes because the said poor subjects, no matter what they do, can neither improve their incomes nor render themselves more solvent." *Raccolta Giunta*, part 1: 116-17. In the 1790's the government nearly abolished the personal tax on the grounds that the peasantry did not constitute an independent source of revenue but only an inconvenient channel by which landlords could be tapped. *La riforma finanziaria*, 447-511. Note also the debate between Pietro Verri and G.R. Carli in the 1770's: Verri, "Meditazioni sull'economia politica (1771)," in *idem*, *"Del piacere e del dolore" ed altre scritti di filosofia ed economia*, ed. R. Felice (Novara, 1964), 240-1; and Carli's annotations in another edition of "Meditations" in *Biblioteca dell'economista*, ser 1, vol 3 (Turin, 1852), 574-5, 630-1.

(55) Romani, *L'agricoltura*, 14-15; Mario Mirri, "Proprietari e contadini toscani nelle riforme leopoldine," *Movimento operaio*, 7 (1955), 198-204; *idem*, "Un inchiesta toscana sui tributi pagati dai mezzadri e sui patti colonici

nella secoi.da metà del settecento," *Annali dell'Istituto Giangiacomo Feltrinelli,* 2 (1959), *passim.*

(56) On the personal tax in general: Neri, *PR,* 206-30; Zaninelli, *Il nuovo censo,* 67-70, 93-6, 156. Zaninelli's explanation (95-6) that the urban leaders of Novara sided with the Giunta simply to ensure that the *personale* fell on rustics instead of city dwellers seems inadequate.

(57) Quoted in Zaninelli, *Il nuovo censo,* 94.

(58) The Giunta memorandum of 7 October 1730, printed in abridgement by Neri, *PR,* 219, 221, 223, 228.

.(59) *PR,* 208.

(60) Neri, *PR,* 224-26.

(61) Neri, *PR,* 226.

(62) Neri, *PR,* 228-9.

(63) In general: Neri, *PR,* 281-323; Zaninelli, *Il nuovo censo,* 98-102.

(64) "Progetto d'autore anonimo fatto alla ECCma. Real Giunta del Nuovo Censimento per la riduzione di tutti le carichi regi esistenti presentatmente nello Stato di Milano a un solo colla fisazione d'un solo metodo uniforme per l'universale ripartimento, e riflessioni della ECCLLma. Congregazione del medesimo Stato in opposto fatte presenti alls stessa ECCELLma. Giunta nel entrante Maggio 1732," in *Miscellanea: Censo ed imposte* (Number 3), paragraphs 2, 16.

(65) Giunta memorandum of 9 May 1733 (abridged) and the "Memorial" (in full) in Neri, *PR,* 289-96, 319-23.

(66) *PR,* 304.

(67) There is no comprehensive study of Neri, and my conclusions are tentative. The biographic details are from Rocchi, "Pompeo Neri," *passim.* For Neri and Pallavicini, Venturi, *Settecento,* 423-9. The following historians claim the importance of Neri at the beginning of Peter Leopold's reign: Adam Wandruszka, *Leopold II* (Vienna, 1963), 1: 167-72; Büchi, *Finanzpolitik,* 149-54; Diaz, *Gianni,* 40-7.

(68) Neri, "Osservazioni sopra il prezzo legale della monete (1751)," in *Scrittori classici, Parte antica* (Milan, 1804), 6: 324-5. The significance of Neri's legal training is stressed by Nucio, biographic appendix, cited note 36 above, xxxiii.

(69) *PR,* 299.

(70) *PR,* 376-7. Valsecchi underlines Neri's administrative skills and empiricism in *L'assolutismo,* 2: 83-4; and in *Storia di Milano,* 12: 284.

(71) See *PR,* 307-10, for Neri's repeated use of the phrase *lo stato in corpo.* On his work in Tuscany, Wandruszka, *Leopold II,* 1: 278; Rocchi, "Pompeo Neri," 56-7, 67, 443; Luigi Dal Pane, *La finanza,* 51; Herman Büchi, *Ein Menschenalter Reformen der Toten Hand in Toscana, 1751-1790* (Berlin, 1912), 27-9, 52-62, 70-2.

(72) Neri, "Discorso sopra lo stato antico e moderno della nobilità di Toscana (1748)," in Ioannis Bonaventurae Neri Badia, *Regiae Celsitudinis Serenissimi Magni Ducis Etruriae in signatura libellorum supplicum gratiae et iustitiae consiliarii Decisiones et responsa iuris. Tomus secundus continens eius dem responsa quibus accedunt Pompeii filii Decisiones responsa et discursus legales* (Florence, 1776), 551-605, 612-13. Neri introduced the essay (p. 550) as being written "in view of the new codification." At the end (p. 643) he stated,

"I leave this information to men better than myself who can draw the conclusions necessary for correcting defects." The phrase "tutor, father and prince" (see below) is in *PR*, 76.

(73) Neri exaggerated the plebian component of Medici agencies. See R. B. Litchfield, "Office-holding in Florence after the Republic," in *Renaissance: Studies in Honor of Hans Baron*, ed. A. Molhe & J. Tedeschi (Florence, 1971), 531-55.

(74) According to Büchi, *Finanzpolitik*, 310, Neri was a leader in the early stage of the Tuscan communal reforms; see also Wandruszka, *Leopold II*, 1: 271. The memoranda of 1763 are discussed and quoted by I. Masetti-Bencini, "Notizie su Pompeo Neri e su alcuni suoi scritti," *Miscellanea storica della Valdelsa*, XXII (1914), 140-6. The grain essay is considered below. The draft program is printed in full by Masetti-Bencini, who dates it 1767 and also mentions the reaction of Peter Leopold ("Notizie," 150-71.) Antonio Anzilotti, "Il tramonto dello stato cittadino," *Archivio storico italiano*, ser 7, vol 1 (1924), 92-3, analyzes the same or a very similar document, dating it 1769. For the assemblies of the 1770's see Mirri, "Proprietari," 183-4.

(75) A convenient edition of the *Discorso* is in *Scrittori classici, Parte moderna*, 1. For useful information about Bandini's life and judgements about lhis work see: Mario Mirri, "Sallustio Antonio Bandini," in *Dizionario biografico degli Italiani* (Rome, 1963), 5: 720-31; Glauco Tozzi, "Sallustio Bandini," in *Memoria della R. Academia nazionale dei Lincei, classe di scienza morali, storiche e filologiche*, ser 6, vol 5 (1933), 69-141; also, Luigi Dal Pane, *La questione del commercio dei grani nel settecento in Italia* (Milan, 1932). 157. Bandini read the nearly complete two volume "Vauban" edition of Boisguillebert; there is controversy about the extent of borrowing. For Boisguillebert himself, see his "Factum de la France (1707)" and "Traité de la Nature, Culture, Commerce et Intérét des Grains (1707)," both in *Economistes-Financiers du XVIIIe Siecle*, ed. E. Daire (Paris, 1843), 286, 289, 304-09, 315-16, 353, 373, 382, 388, 392.

(76) On Bandini and Neri: Rochi, "Pompeo Neri," 52, 57; Venturi, *Settecento*, 53; idem, *Illuministi italiani*, also edited by Venturi (Milan-Naples, 1958), 3: 888-9; Dal Pane, *La questione*, 175-6; Nuccio, biographic appendix, lxxii; Mirri, "Bandini," 723, 729-30. These authors agree, with more or less caution, that Bandini left his mark on Neri.

(77) Rocchi, "Pompeo Neri," 58, 264-5; Büchi, *Finanzpolitik*, 150, 154-69; Dal Pane, *La questione*, 177-81; Nuccio, biographic appendix, lxxiv; Wandruszka, *Leopold II*, 1: 187-9; Diaz, *Gianni*, 40-3. The role of Peter Leopold in legislating on grain was also crucial.

(78) Venturi, speaking for himself and quoting others, calls Neri's thought and personality neat, clear, restrained, prudent and nobly calm: *Illuministi*, 3: 945, 949; Wandruszka, *Leopold II*, 1: 188, states that the programs and ideas of Neri in the 1760's were "long cherished."

(79) Neri, "Sopra la materia frumentaria," in *Scrittori classici* (Milan, 1816), 49 (*Supplimento*), 17-18, 25, 33-4, 37-8, 40-1; idem, "Memoria sulla mendicita," in *Illuministi*, 3: 972-3, 975-7. On the origins and immediate impact of "Sopra," see Büchi, *Finanzpolitik*, 150-4; Wandrsuzka, *Leopold II*, 1: 187-9. For examples of Bandini's different approach, see his *Discorso*, 245, 248-9, 255-7.

(80) Venturi, *Settecento*, 432.

(81) The *mercimonio*: Neri, *PR*, 188-205; *Raccolta Giunta*, part 1: 82, 86-8, 97, 120-4; G.R. Carli, "Osservazioni sulla riforma del mercimonio (1769)," in *Saggi inediti di G.R. Carli*, 90-3, 115; Pietro Verri, letter to Ilario Corte, 2 Sept. 1769, in *Lettere e scritti inediti*, ed. Carlo Casati (Milan, 1881), 4: 115; Sebastiani, *La tassazione degli ecclesiastici*, 52. The *personale*: G.R. Carli, "Relazione del Censimento," 256-8; *idem*, "Saggio di economia pubblica," 81-3; *Raccolta Provisionale Delegazione*, 20; *La Riforma finanzaria*, 467-8.

(82) Neri, *PR*, 347-9; Romani, *L'agricoltura*, 19, 99-105; Cattaneo, *Scritti economici*, 3: 156, 169-71.

(83) Carli, "Relazione del Censimento," 241-4; also p. 15 above.

(84) The formal freezing of assessments is discussed below. Carli, "Saggio di economia pubblica (1768)," 32, stressed the advance of prices since the 1720's, claiming that in the 1760's wheat was fluctuating between 28 and 37 *lira* per *moggio*. For more on prices see Vianello, *Il settecento*, 312; Cesare Beccaria, *Opere*, ed. S. Romagnoli (Florence, 1958), 2: 232-3; Romani, *L'agricoltura*, 85-93. On agriculture after 1760, *Storia di Milano*, 12: 525-7; Venturi, *Settecento*, 441-2; Caizzi, *Industria*, 94-5.

(85) *La riforma finanzaria*, xvii, xxvii; *Storia di Milano*, 12: 287-8; Carli, "Relazione del Censimento," 247, 251; *idem*, "Saggio di economia pubblica," 59-60, 76-7; *idem*, "Osservazioni sulla riforma del mercimonio," 95; *Raccolta Provisionale Delegazione*, 20; Caizzi, *Industria*, 170-1. The *scudo*, a money of account, equalled 6 *lira* or 1,440 *denari*.

(86) Forbonnois, "Précis historique du cadastre," 258; Carli, "Saggio di economia pubblica," 32.

(87) Vianello, *Settecento*, 255; Dandolo, *Sulle cause dell'avvilimento delle nostre granaglie e sulle industrie agrarie riparatrici dei danni che ne derivano* (Milan, 1820), 96 (note 1).

(88) Romani, *L'agricoltura*, 85-9; Dandolo, *Sulle cause*, 114-16; Cattaneo, "Notizie naturali e civili su la Lombardia (1844)," in *Scritti storici e geografici*, 1: 416.

(89) *PR*, 98-9.

(90) Carli, letter to Neri (1771) in *Scrittori classici*, *Parte moderna*, 14: 384, 387.

(91) Freganeschi, "Disertazione," cited note 49 above, no pagination. Freganeschi describes the *Ducato* paper, which I have not seen.

(92) Romani, *L'agricoltura*, 85-93, 112-18, 163-71, 193-9; *idem*, "L'agricoltura lodigiana e la 'nuova agricoltura' del settecento," *Archivio storico lombardo*, ser 8, vol 8 (1958), 184-92; Emilio Sereni, *Storia del paessaggio agrario italiano*, (Bari, 1962), 178-81.

(93) Carli, "Saggio di economia pubblica," 41.

(94) Sebastiani, *La tassazione degli ecclesiastici*, cited note 24 above, 9, 14, 18, 63.

(95) *Raccolta Giunta*, cited note 20 above, part 2: 114-15.

(96) Neri, "Memoria per servire alle istruzione da darsi, quando si risolva la trattazione del proposto concordato con la corte di Roma (1757)," in Sebastiani, *La tassazione degli ecclesiastici*, 34, 39.

(97) "Relazione di ciò che ha pensato al Gunta sopra il censimento di coloni (1757)," in Sebastiani, *La tassazione degli ecclesiastici*, 60-1; also 53-4.

(98) Sebastiani, *La Tassazione degli ecclesiastici*, 11-18; Valsecchi, *L'assolutismo*, 2: 330-4; *Storia di Milano*, 12: 509-15; Rocchi, "Pompeo Neri," 257-9. Sebastiani judges the tariff negotiations of small importance and no excuse for the weakness of the concordat. Caizzi, *Industria*, 107, 115-20, 215-41, places the same commercial treaty in a more positive context: though not in itself especially fruitful, it was part of a sustained effort by Vienna to aid the Lombard economy, the results of which were finally excellent.

(99) *Raccolta Provisionale Delegazione*, cited note 24 above, 27-33.

(100) *Raccolta Magistrato Camerale*, cited note 24 above, 33-4. With this imposition the government at last admitted its true position on the church immunity, calling the 200,000 *lira*, "un vero carico reale" and allowing church owners, individual or corporate, to participate, with the same rights as any laic owner, in the councils of the jurisdiction in which a property was located. *Raccolta Magistrato Camerale*, 36, 46-7. Earlier documents in this collection and in *Raccolta Provisionale Delegazione* contain hints rather than explanations of royal poliy. Carli, who obviously knew better, also gave an obscure and inaccurate description of the concordat in his "Relazione del Censimento," 262-4. Perhaps the mystification was intentional to save face for the church.

(101) The exemption granted by the condordat was slightly higher than I have indicated because peasants on immune lands paid only 6 *lira* for the personal tax instead of the usual 7. On the other hand the concordat left unstated the fact that the Austrians would make leaseholders (commercial farmers) on immune properties pay almost the full land tax. Presumedly the church had to accept a lower lease price to compensate for this expense, just as it probably took higher rents from the peasants in return for their reduced personal tax. Leaseholders on laic land paid no real tax. *Raccolta Giunta*, part 2: 115; *Raccolta Provisionale Delegazione*, 8, 20, 32-5; Sebastiani, *La tassazione degli ecclesiastici*, 66-7. Curiously Neri anticipated the actual working of the church immunity in his memorandum of 1757: "The use of the term 'colonica' does not disturb me because words cause no injury when they leave unchanged the substance of an obligation. One may employ the term in the new system, provided that it does not place any fiscal burden on the peasants, nor diminish the responsibility of the church lands to pay half the tax." At the time this statement represented only a hope and most of the paper was devoted to the evil consequences which would follow from establishing a true *colonica*. Sebastiani, *La tassazione degli ecclesiastici*, 40.

(102) "Duplica della Provincia del Ducato alla Eccelsa. Real Giunta de Cinque Delegati (1743?)," in *Miscellanea: Censo ed imposte* (number 1), cited note 49 above, paragraphs 204-12, 218-19, 232-9, 364, 373-80; and the attached document F: "Dimostrazione, che la Pertica Rurale paga molta più della Civile della stressa qualità e censimento." The quote is from the latter.

(103) "Della Sindaci Generali del Ducato per la Distribuzione Proporzionata del Carico Personale Desiderata da tutto lo Stato di Milano contra La Generale Egaluaglianza voluta in Forma Capitazione dal solo sig. Oratore di Cremona (6 March 1753)," *passim;* Giovanni Montorfani, "Per la Provincia del Ducato in riposta alla Confutazione del Signor Marchese Fraganeschi, Oratore di Cremona, intorno al Metodo della Distribuzione del Carico Personale Forense (4 August 1753)," *passim;* also the *Ducato* pamphlet which is reproduced

without a title or date in "Rilievi delli Rappresentanti li Pubblici di Cremona, Lodi, Pavia e Casal Maggiore al di contro Memoriale del Ducato (1758)," no pagination. These short pieces are in *Miscellanea: Censo ed imposte* (number 1). Freganeschi is spelt with an "a" or an "e".

(104) "Riflessioni contro al nuovo Progetto insinutata all E.R.G. del Censimento di staccare dal Ducato alcuni Territori ed Aggregarli ad altre Provincie (15 June 1754)," 15, in *Miscellanea: Censo ed imposte* (number 1). "The original owners of the *Ducato* have among others the privilege of being inscribed in the Noble Orders of the Principal City." As already noted, the major prerequisite for admission to the Milanese patriciate was that the family had lived nobly for over a century in the city or its territory.

(105) Valsecchi, *L'assolutismo*, 2: 64-5.

(106) "Rilieve delli Rappresentanti." The representatives printed the *Ducato* pamphlet in full and then placed their own comments in the margins.

(107) *Carteggio di Pietro e di Alessandro Verri*, cited note 8 above, 1 (part 2): 43; Valsecchi, *L'assolutismo*, 2: 312-13; Carlo Angelo Conigliani, *G.B. Freganeschi e le questioni tributarie in Lombardia nel secola XVIII* (Modena, 1898), *passim* (48 pp.). It is Conigliani who mentions Freganeschi's family.

(108) Conigliani, *G.B. Fraganeschi*. Actually Conigliani discusses three essays but one of them, published in 1750 on the subject of the personal tax, seemingly adds nothing of interest. The other two are: *Progetto del Marchese Giovan Battista Fraganeschi, Oratore della Città di Cremona, col quale, togliendo con vantaggio del Principe varii ostacoli alle arti, alle manifatture, al commercio e all'agricoltura, verrebbe il carico ad essere con solievo universale distribuito più proporzionatamente del Nuovo Generale Censimento e di qualunque altro metodo che potesse idearsi ed esegiursi* (Milan, 1759); *Testamento economico-politico di un patrizio lombardo invecchiato negli affari pubblici* (1787). Conigliani is certain that Freganeschi wrote the last work though it appeared anonymously and some have attributed it to his father. I have seen none of these publications.

(109) "Delli Sindaci Generali" *passim;* Montorfani, "Per la Provincia," *passim.* These opposing statements quote from and describe in detail the Freganeschi pamphlets, which I have not seen.

(110) Freganeschi, "Disertazione." Montorfani, "Per la Provincia," 4, gives the dating of the enumeration essay.

(111) Neri, *PR*, 72-81; the quote, 79. See also note 51 above. Compare Carlo Morandi, *Idee e formazione politiche in Lombardia dal 1748 al 1814* (Turin, 1927), 34, 46: "So (in Lombardy) there gradually developed a small group of medium proprietors belonging to the middle class, men for the most part who began as administrators and exactors, whereby they had accumulated the capital they now invested in land . . . In the Kingdom of Naples was lacking . . . that rural bourgeoisie which had given 18th century Lombardy a new element of social life, a provocation and justification for agricultural and economic reforms." Similarly Antonio Anzilotti once claimed that the reformist writings of Sallustio Bandini reflected the aspirations of a Tuscan rural bourgeoisie. Anzilotti, "Stato e chiesa in Toscana (1911)," in *idem, Movimenti e contrasti per l'unità italiana* (Milan, 1964), 185-7. But recently Mario Mirri has pointed out that no evidence substantiates even the existence of this class, let alone its central significance. He contends more cogently that the period of Peter Leopold was one of growing noble power which lasted well into

the 19th century. Mirri, "Proprietari," cited note 55 above, 176-7, 220-1.

(112) I know of no study about rural government in Lombardy which could supplement or correct Neri. A Giunta memorandum of 28 May 1733 (*PR,* 119) mentioned councils composed of large sharecroppers (*massari*) and leaseholders, as did the anonymous pamphlet cited on pp. 22-3 above. The social and political inferiority of rural officials was a major theme of the *Ducato* paper discussed on p. 39 above. In contrast one modern historian states without documentation that most of the community representatives were noblemen: Franco Catalano, *Illuministi,* cited note 5 above, 81.

(113) See below 59-62.

(114) Corrado Vivanti, *Le campagne del Mantovano,* cited note 8 above, 74.

(115) Rosario Villari, *Mezzogiorno e contadini nell'età moderna (Bari, 1961),* 90-9.

(116) *Raccolta Giunta,* part 1: 70-3.

(117) *Raccolta Giunta,* part 2: 3-52; the quote, 4-5.

(118) These estimates of land distribution are from Romani, *L'agricoltura,* 58-60. The quote is from *Raccolta Giunta,* part 2: 8.

(119) On the dependence of peasant owners see Pugliese, "Condizione economiche," cited note 5 above, 75. The figures on land distribution tell much of the story. In the mountains, where one fifth of the population lived, land was fairly equally divided, but in the populous hills and plains 80% of the owners held only 15% of the land surface under cultivation. Romani, *L'agricoltura,* 23, 58-60.

(120) For details on the convocation see *Raccolta Giunta,* part 2: 7-10. Implementation of the communal reform law is discussed below, 73-5.

(121) Cattaneo, "Sulle legge communale e provinciale (1864)," in *Scritti politici,* cited note 4 above, 4: 418, 423.

(122) *Raccolta Giunta,* part 2: 3-4, 7, 10-11, 18-21; the quote, 19.

(123) *Raccolta Giunta,* part 2: 32-5; the quote, 32.

(124) *Raccolta Giunta,* part 2: 12-17 (*personale*); 17-18 (*mercimoniale*).

(125) Cattaneo, "Sulle legge," 62; Verri, "Memorie storiche sulla economia pubblica dello Stato di Milano (1768)," in *Scrittori classici italiani di economia politica, Parte moderna,* cited note 2 above, 17: 160; Carli, "Relazione del Censimento," cited note 2 above, 275.

(126) Preliminary instructions for compiling rolls and electing deputies were issued for the *personale* on 24 May and for the *mercimoniale* on 25 May 1754. *Raccolta Giunta,* part 1: 79-88. New information on the commercial tax, regulating rates of payment according to categories of wealth, appeared on 23 Sept. 1754 (p. 97). The personal tax became law on 5 December 1755, the commercial tax on 19 December of the same year (pp. 116-23). The May edicts provided these interesting examples for the guidance of the property deputies (pp. 81-2): "Francisco Torni pretends to be exempt from the personal tax because he is 60 years, but he has produced no evidence . . . Antonio Falleri, number 41 on the personal roll, has been described as a cabinetmaker, but since his work is scarce and irregular, and his income is tenuous, the deputies agree that he should be considered a simple hardworker (and not liable to the commercial tax)." The quote in my text is from p. 80.

(127) *Raccolta Giunta,* part 2: 13-14, 17; *Raccolta Provisionale Delegazione,* 45-8. The one *lira* reduction was given to renters and relatives living in their houses while hired hands paid the full amount.

(128) *Raccolta Giunta,* part 2: 8, 13-16; the long quote, 15.

(129) This paragraph is based on *Raccolta Giunta,* part 2: 38-44; the quote, 38. See also Carli, "Relazione del Censimento," 314.

(130) For Lombard feudalism see note 16 above. In April of 1765 the directors of the Censimento asked chancellors to inventory their districts for information about feudal claims against communes, having ordered all title holders to present their documents in Milan. The intention was to accept legal claims and disqualify doubtful ones. *Raccolta Magistrato Camerale,* 21-2. The sample communal budget of 1760 described a commune with a capital value of 50,000 *scudi* which paid annually about 40 *lira* in feudal dues *(censi)* and 50 *lira* for the salary of the *podesta.* I believe that the listing of 20 *lira* for *fante, or sia Barigello* was also a feudal expense. *Raccolta Provisionale Delegazione,* 50-2.

(131) *Raccolta Giunta,* part 2: 43.

(132) Verri, "Memorie storiche," 164-5. For Verri's different views of a later period see below 63-4. In 1769, in another context, he spoke of the chancellors as "poor folk with scarcely enough to live on." Letter to Ilario Corte, 2 Sept. 1769, in *Lettere e scritti inediti,* cited note 81 above, 4: 118.

(133) Carli, "Relazione del Censimento," 276-7. In 1780 Carli instructed royal inspectors on how to evaluate the performance of chancellors. The brief analysis of communal politics which he included was characteristically obscure. "In deciding upon the worth of a chancellor be sure that your facts come from 'legitimate sources.' Men in this kind of work often are hated just for the zeal with which they enforce the laws. Conversely they are sometimes favored because they neglect the laws and further the private interests of the most powerful and authoritative persons in the community. Nothing is more pernicious for communal administration than factions, faction leaders and litigious troublemakers; and the consequences of their actions are still worse if the chancellor supports them, and especially if he associates himself with the exactor." *Raccolta Magistrato Camerale,* 79-80.

(134) Valsecchi, *L'assolutismo,* cited note 7 above, 2: 342.

(135) *Raccolta Provisionale Delegazione,* 15.

(136) *Raccolta Provisionale Delegazione,* 24.

(137) This and the next two paragraphs are based on the reform acts in *Raccolta Giunta,* part 2: 53-60 (Cremona); 61-9 (Pavia); 69-72 (Casal Maggiore); 73-8 (Como); 118-23 (Lodi); 128-31 (Milan). Also interesting is Ettore Verga, *I consigli del commune di Milano* (no place, no date), 14-28.

(138) The statute for Casal Maggiore was typical: "The prefects of sanitation, canals, streets and victualing will continue to be elected in the usual way by the (patrician) Council General, the present reform intending no novelty in these matters." The patricians also held their authority over the office of commercial taxes (*camera del mercimonio*). In Pavia for instance the patrician council elected four of its own members to sit on the chamber and selected four more commercial members from a list of eight submitted to it by the guilds.

(139) Verga, *I consigli,* 26-7.

(140) Carli, "Relazione del Censimento," 282-9; the quote, 285.

(141) Verri, "Memoria cronologica dei cambiamenti pubblici dello Stato di Milano, 1750-1795," in *Lettere e scritti inediti,* 4: 363-4. The complex evolution of Verri's thought cannot be discussed here, but the following remarks to his brother, written in November and December of 1771, are indicative. "I no longer have the sentiments of yesterday about our country, nor

would I see with pleasure the humliation of the (Milanese) nobility . . . It would be an evil without compensation to annihilate the civil corps which alone has the right to inform the throne of the needs of the land, and which may place limits on the power of royal ministers only so long as it can warn the sovereign of abuses . . . This class of men, unarmed, must obey first of all; but it must also expose disorders . . ." *Carteggio di Pietro e di Alessandro Verri,* 4: 274, 297. A more comprehensive statement is in Pietro's long letter of the same period (undated) which described his recent stay in Vienna: *Carteggio,* 4: 311-42. See also Nino Valeri, *Pietro Verri*(Milan, 1937), chapter 16. By the time he wrote the "Chronological Memoir" Verri believed that a constitutional assembly of notables was a better safeguard against royal despotism than patrician privilege, but in the 1750's no such option existed, not even on the horizon. See below, 63-5, 72-3.

(142) Carpani, "Discorso storico dell'origine e cambiamento del Consiglio dei LX Decurioni (e) del Tribunale di Provisione da primi tempi della repubblica milanese sino al 1760, cioè alla pubblicazione del Censimento (1771)," in *Economisti minori del settecento lombardo,* ed., C.A. Vianello (Milan, 1942), *passim* (145-72); *idem,* "Discorsi sopra lo Stato di Milano (1770)," in *Economisiti minori,* 136-7, 144. If Carpani was frank Carli dissembled, for he too, in the 1760's, feared that the Milanese patriciate might use its control of the city government to turn the masses against the Censimento. At the time Vienna was moving against the nobles, though without much success. See below 71-2. Finally in 1784-6 the resolute Joseph II appointed men of the middle classes to the patrician councils, which also lost some of their authority. This departure from the work of Maria Theresa was in turn reversed by Leopold II. Verga, *I consigli,* 25-8.

(143) *Raccolta Giunta,* part 2: 37.

(144) Note the revealing and misleading remarks of Carli: "One example is sufficient to illustrate these reforms — that of Cremona." "This principle of uniting the various groups . . . forming a sort of parliament composed of decurions, provincials (*provinciali*) and merchants (*mercanti*) . . . regulated all the reforms of the cities . . . and so it is superfluous to give more details." Carli, "Relazione del Censimento," 276-7, 283.

(145) *Raccolta Giunta,* part 2: 191.

(146) The amendments, the basis for this and the following two paragraphs, are in *Raccolta Giunta,* part 2: 131-90; The Varese quote, 133.

(147) *Persona civile e polita, nè di condizione rustica, mecanica o servile.*

(147a) Seventeen charters installed personal and commercial deputies on the councils, generally explaining their functions with a reference to the law of 1755. Verese, Monza, Tiviglio and Gravedona offered this statement: "The personal and commercial deputies, though entering the convocations, are neither capable of deliberative votes nor have any of the prerogatives belonging to the major taxpayers . . ." *Raccolta Giunta,* part 2: 136, 144, 159, 190.

(148) *Raccolta Giunta,* part 2: 158.

(149) Franco Catalano, "Aspetti della vita economico-sociale lombardia nel secolo XVIII," in *Illuministi,* cited note 5 above, 86-9; also see below 79-80.

(150) *Raccolta Giunta,* part 2: 158 (Triviglio), 188 (Gravedona), 171 (Castel-Leone).

(151) See above, 28-9, 56, 60.

(152) Valsecchi, *L'assolutismo,* 2: 334.

(153) *PR*, 317-18. As mentioned on p. 1 above (ref. note 3 above), in the 1790's the Congregation members called the land tax "the fruit of intense labor by the most intelligent officials . . . the best of its type in Europe."

(154) Louis Philippe May, "Despotisme légal et despotisme éclairé," cited note 10 above, 58-62, says of Mercier de La Riiere, who despised every kind of deliberative assembly, that his motto could have been. "The king reigns and the law governs."

(155) Verri, "Pensiere sullo stato politico del Milanese nel 1790," in *Scritti vari*, ed. G. Carcano (Florence, 1854), 2: appendix, 3-38; especially, 21-3, 28, 30-6; the quotes, 32, 33-4. At the time Verri presented his views orally to the Council of Sixty, the essay not being published until long after.

(156) *Storia di Milano*, 12: 320-29; Carli, "Saggio di economia publica," cited note 14 above, 42-50; Francesco de Stefano, "G.R. Carli e il Consiglio supremo dell'economia a Milano," *Rivista storica italiana*, ser 4, vol. 4 (1933), 471-4. In July of 1761 the Temporary Commission dissolved and its work fell to the Cameral Magistracy, but this tribunal, though created in 1749, was not the fresh and responsive instrument sought by the Austrians for grand projects. *Raccolta Magistrato Camerale*, 1; *Storia di Milano*, 12: 282-4.

(157) In addition to the materials cited immediately above, see the edict of 20 November 1765 in *La riforma finanzaria*, cited note 3 above, 5-17.

(158) *La riforma finanzaria*, 17.

(159) "Trecentosessantasei lettere di Gian Rinaldo Carli," ed. Baccio Ziliotto, in *Archeografo Triestino*, ser 3, vol 5 (1909), 30-1. Hereafter "366 lettere."

(160) These biographic details are from Francesco de Stefano, *G.R. Carli* (Modena, 1942), 9-10, 15, 18, 24, 81; Venturi, *Illuministi italiani*, cited note 76 above, 3: 419, 421-7; Baccio Ziliotto, "Primi moti antioligarchi a Capodistria," *Archivio Veneto*, ser 5, vols 54-5 (1954): 71. Carli's writings on money are as follows: *Delle monete e dell'istituzione delle zecche d'Italia*, vol 1 (Mantua, 1754), vol 2 (Pisa, 1757), vol 3 (Lucca, 1760). Two early works are: "Sull'impiego del danaro (1747)," in Carli, *Opere* (Milan, 1784-94), 1: 1-47; *Dell'origine e del commercio della moneta e dell'istituzione delle zecchi d'Italia* (Venice, 1751).

(161) "366 lettere," 5 (1909): 27, 43; and 12, 32-3, 37-9, 286. See also vol. 4 (1908) of the letters, 78-101; and de Stefano, *G.R. Carli*, 15-16.

(162) "366 lettere," 4 (1908): 91-2, 97-8.

(163) Ziliotto, "Primi moti," *passim* (71-9); Karl J. Beloch, *Bevölkerungsgeschichte Italiens* (Berlin, 1937-61), 3: 28-9.

(164) "366 lettere," 4: 78-84; the long quote, 84.

(165) Ziliotto, "Primi moti." *passim;* "366 lettere," 5(1909): 61-4.

(166) Carli, "l'Uomo libero (1778)," in *Opere*, 18: 54-55, 108-39, 161-79, 180-97, 201-02, 205-06, 234-7, 251; the quoted sentence, 177. On the composition of the book, which was intended as a refutation of Rousseau, see de Stefano, *G.R. Carli*, 30. In two earlier works of Carli these interesting remarks appear: "We must remember that the government of the Greeks was democratic . . . and that plays would have had small success had they not represented . . . or interested the people. This explains the necessity of the chorus, which . . . seems superfluous to us because in our day it would be inconvenient, if not ridiculous, for great affairs and political matters to be treated

in public and in the presence of the people who would not hesitate to give advice and counsel . . . We must consider if the norms of a democratic period are still valid and indispensible in Europe where the people are excluded and detached from all involvement in public affairs.'' ''Dell'indole del teatro tragico antico e moderno (1744-46),'' in *Opere*, 17: 155-6.

''The nobility: this group which is respectable and necessary to the state; which acts as a link between prince and people; which aids the arts, manufacturing and commerce through its luxury; which with its dignity and authority helps to quiet the plebians; and which . . . can do such good for humanity; this nobility is numerous and illustrious.'' ''Saggio politico ed economico sopra la Toscana (1757),'' in *Opere*, 1: 335-6.

(167) Carli, ''Nuovo metodo per le scuole pubbliche di Italia (1774),'' in *Opere*, 18: 280.

(168) See above, 56-7.

(169) de Stefano, *G.R. Carli*, 178.

(170) de Stefano, *G.R. Carli*, 181, 193, 238, 240; Umberto Marcelli, ''Il carteggio Carli-Kaunitz (1765-1793),'' *Archivio storico italiano*, vol 113 (1955) 553-4, 556, 559-60, 565, 571; the quotes, 553, 560.

(171) ''Carteggio Carli-Kaunitz,'' 393.

(172) ''Carteggio Carli-Kaunitz,'' 577; de Stefano, *G.R. Carli*, 251-2. The essay is ''Saggio di economia pubblica,'' cited many times above.

(173) ''Saggio di economia pubblica,'' 3-7, 11-30; the quote, 29-30. Carli was slightly mistaken about the evolution of the General Council: see Verga, *I consigli*, cited note 137 above, 14-15, 19.

(174) *Carteggio di Pietro e di Alessandro Verri*, 1, part 2: 146.

(175) *Carteggio di Pietro e di Alessandro Verri*, 1, part 2: 185-6.

(176) *Carteggio di Pietro e di Alessandro Verri*, 1, part 2: 330, 335; vol 2: 348; Verri, *Lettere e scritti inediti*, 3: 350-1; vo 4; 86-7.

(177) *Lettere e scritti inediti*, 4: 50; *Carteggio di Pietro e di Alessandro Verri*, 4: 315-16, 318, 320, 328, 339-40; the quote, 339-40; see also note 141 above.

(178) See for example *Storia di Milano*, 12: 309-10, 330-33.

(179) The president of the Magistracy in 1758, Marchese Mantegazza, was one of the men whom Neri called a vandal; and in 1760 Firmian told Kauntiz that of the ten members of the tribunal only three were reliable. Valsecchi quotes Firmian but nontheless gives his own opinion, without argument, that the Magistracy acted toward the Censimento no differently than the Neri Giunta. In an order of 9 January 1764 the Magistracy acknowleded the ''superior determination'' of Firmian. *Storia di Milano*, 12: 515; Valsecchi, *L'assolutismo*, 2: 96, 334, 336, 340; *Raccolta Magistrato Camerale*, 15. This Cameral Magistracy should not be confused with the new agency of the same name which in the 1770's, under Carli's leadership, absorbed the duties of the Economic Council and the mixed farm commission.

(180) *Raccolta Magistrato Camerale*, 7-12 (15 February 1762 and 8 March 1763), 18-20 (10 December 1764); the quotes, 10-11.

(181) *Raccolta Magistrato Camerale*, 15 (9 January 1764), 18-20 (10 December 1764); the quotes, 18-19. The limitation of one term for property deputies did not apply to the first deputy for the obvious reason that only three owners in any jurisdiction, the three with the highest assessments, were eligible for the post. *Raccolta Magistrato Camerale*, 113.

(182) *Raccolta Magistrato Camerale,* 77-8 (14 June 1780).

(183) *Raccolta Magistrato Camerale,* 72-3, 103-04; the same collection contains many reports of improprieties and difficulties in the period after 1764: 25-6, 29, 32-3, 75, 78-83. In September of 1770 Kaunitz complimented the Economic Council for its "firm maintenance and execution of the census." de Stefano, *G.R. Carli,* 265.

(184) Pietro Verri, "Meditazione sull'economia politica, con annotazioni di Gianrinaldo Carli," in *Scrittori classici, Parte moderna,* cited note 2 above, vol. 15: 61-4, 218-31, 234-5. For evidence that Carli was the author of the annotations, which appeared anonymously, see de Stefano, *G.R. Carli, 138-9; Carteggio di Pietro e di Alessandro Verri,* 4: 263-4, 278.

(185) Carli, "Relazione del Censimento," cited note 2 above, 273-90; "Carteggio Carli-Kaunitz," vol 114 (1956), 126.

(186) *Considerazioni sull'annona dello Stato di Milano nel XVIII secolo,* ed. C.A. Vianello (Milan, 1940), *passim;* pp. 3-168 cover the period 1767-8; pp. 169-74 reproduce Carli's letter to Firmian; pp. 176-333 cover the period 1773-1793. The report of February 1768 is in de Stefano, *G.R. Carli,* 247-50. See also Carli's letter to Neri, of September 1771, cited note 90 above, 363-99; especially 375, 385.

(187) de Stefano, *G.R. Carli,* 261-3.

(188) Carli, "Delle lettere americane (1777-80)," in *Opere,* 11: 151-3, 260-92; *idem,* "l'Uomo libero," 177.

(189) Renato Mori, "Il movimento reazionario in Toscana alle riforme economiche leopoldine nel 1790," *Archivio storico italiano,* 100 (1942), *passim,;* Diaz, *Gianni,* cited note 28 above, 338-9; Francesco Gianni, "Memoria sul tumulto accaduto in Firenze il di' 9 Giugno 1790 (1793)," in *Scrittori di pubblica economia* (Florence, 1848-9), 1: 209-65.

(190) Verri, "Meditazione . . . con annotazioni," 95-6.

(191) Carli, "Osservazioni sulla riforma del mercimonio (1769)," cited note 81 above, 88-9, 108-15.

(192) Venturi, *Illuministi italiani,* 3: 428-31.

(193) Verri, "Meditazione . . . con annotazioni," 266, 322-3.

(194) de Stefano, *G.R. Carli,* 264-5.

(195) *Considerazioni sull'annona,* 242, 44.

(196) Unless otherwise noted, the following discussion, including quotations, is taken from Catalano, "Aspetti della vita economico-sociale lombardia nel secolo XVIII," in *Illuministi,* cited note 5 above, 77-101.

(197) *Raccolta Magistrato Camerale,* 13-4.

(198) In February of 1765 Carli wrote to Girolamo Gravisi, "If the peasants do not attend to the water and dig the ditches and pathways in the fields they have no claim on subsistence." In September, in a letter to Giuseppe Gravisi, he spoke more generally of the "ignorant laziness of our barbarous peasants, who resist each new improvement." "366 lettere," 4(1908); 97; 5(1909): 27.

(199) The figures on communal property are in Romani, *L'agricoltura,* 53-6. In 1773 Beccaria recommended selling off mountain commons but on the advice of Carli and others the monarchy, then and later, refused.

(200) *Raccolta Magistrato Camerale,* 55-6.

(201) *Raccolta Magistrato Camerale,* 56: "Whoever obliges himself to cultivate most quickly the portion of moors or uncultivated lands, to the acquisition of which he aspires, will be preferred to all other qualified buyers."

(202) Venturi, *Settecento riformatore,* cited note 5 above, 686-7.

BIBLIOGRAPHY

A: 18th and early 19th century materials.

Badini, Salustio, "Discorso sopra la Maremma di Siena (1737)," in *Scrittori classici italiani di economia politica, Parte moderna,* ed. P. Custodi, Vol. 1. Milan: Destefanis, 1803.

Beccaria, Cesare, *Opere,* ed. S. Romagnoli, Vol. 2. Florence: Sansoni, 1958.

Boisguillebert, Pierre Le Pesant de, "Factum de la France (1707)," and "Traité de la nature, culture, commerce et intérét des grains (1707)," in *Economistes-Financiers du XVIIIe siecle,* ed. E. Daire. Paris: Guillaumin, 1843.

Carli, Gianrinaldo, "Del libero commercio de'grani: lettera al Presidente Pompeo Neri (1771)," in *Scrittori classici italiani di economia politica, Parte moderna,* ed. P. Custodi, Vol. 14. Milan: Destefanis, 1804.

Idem, Opere, 19 Vols. Milan: Imperial Monistero di S. Ambrogio Maggiore, 1784-1794. Contains: "Sull'impiego del danaro (1747)," Vol. 1. "Saggio politico ed economico sopra la Toscana (1757)," Vol. 1. "Delle monete e dell'istituzione delle zecche d'Italia (1754-1760)," Vols. 2-7. "Delle lettere americane (1777-1780)," Vols. 11-14. "Dell'indole del teatro tragico antico e moderno (1744-1746)," Vol. 17. "L'uomo libero (1778)," Vol. 18. "Nuovo metodo per le scuole pubbliche di Italia (1774)," Vol. 18.

Idem, "Osservazioni sulla riforma del mercimonio (1769)," and "Saggio di economia pubblica (1768)," in *Saggi inediti di Gian Rinaldo Carli,* ed., C.A. Vianello. Florence: Olschki, 1938.

Idem, "Relazione del Censimento (1784)," in *Scrittori classici italiani di economia politica, Parte moderna,* ed. P. Custodi, Vol. 14. Milan: Destefanis, 1804.

Idem, 'Trecento sessantasei lettere di Gian Rinaldo Carli," ed. B. Ziliotto, *Archeografo Triestino,* Ser. 3, Vols. 4-7 (1908-1913). Abbreviated as "366 lettere."

Carpani, Francesco, "Discorsi sopra lo Stato di Milano (1770)" and "Discorso storico dell'origine e cambiamento del Consiglio dei LX Decurioni (e) del Tribunale di Provisione da'primi tempi della republica milanese sino al 1760, cioè alla publicazione del censimento (1771)," in *Economisti minori del settecento lombardo,* ed. C.A. Vianello. Milan: Giuffrè, 1942.

Considerazioni sull'annona dello Stato di Milano nel XVIII secolo, ed. C.A. Vianello. Milan: Giuffrè, 1940.

Dandolo, Vincenzo, *Sulle cause dell'avvilimento delle nostre granaglie e sulle industrie agrarie riparatrici dei danni che ne derivano.* Milan: Sonzogno, 1820.

Forbonnais, François Véron de, "Précis historique du cadastre établi dans le duchè de Milan," in *Principes et observations economiques,* Vol. 2. Amsterdam: Rey, 1767.

Gaudin, Martin-Michel (Duc de Gaëte), ''Mémoire sur le cadastre (1818),'' in *Supplément aux mémoires et souvenirs.* Paris: Goetschy, 1834.

Gianni, Francesco, ''Memoria sul tumulto accaduto in Firenze il di'9 Giugno 1790 (1793),'' in *Scrittori di pubblica economia,* Vol. 1. Florence: Niccolai, 1848.

Lupi, Carlo, *Storia de 'principi, delle massime e regole seguite nelle formazione del catasto prediale introdotto nello Stato di Milano l'anno 1760.* Milan: I.R. Stamperia, 1825.

Marcelli, Umberto, ''Il carteggio Carli-Kaunitz, 1765-1793,'' *Archivio storico italiano,* Vols. 113-114 (1955-1956).

Miscellanea: Censo ed imposte, Nr. 1. A bound, unpaginated volume in the Biblioteca Nazionale Braidenese of Milan.

Contains: ''Rilievi delli Rappresentanti li Pubblici di Cremona, Lodi, Pavia e Casal Maggiore al di contro Memoriale del Ducato (1758),''

''Duplica della Provincia del Ducato alla Eccelsa. Real Giunta de Cinque Delegati (1743?).''

''Delli Sindaci Generali del Ducato per la Distribuzione Proporzionata del Carico Personale Desiderata da tutto lo Stato di Milano contra La Generale Egaluaglianza voluta in Forma Capitazione dal solo sig. Oratore di Cremona (6 March 1753).''

''Riflessioni contro al nuovo Progretto insinuata all E.R. G. del Censimento di staccare dal Ducato alcuni Territori ed Aggregarli ad altre Provincie (15 June 1754).''

Montorfani, Giovanni, ''Per la Provincia del Ducato in riposta all Confutazione del Signor Marchese Freganeschi, Oratore di Cremona, intorno al Metodo della Distribuzione del Carico Personale Forense (4 August 1753).''

Anonymous, ''Le piante de Moroni e d'altri fruitti considerate nel soggetto del Generale Censimento ovvero Discorso practico-legale nella questione (1726?).''

Freganeschi, Giambattista, ''Dissertazione del Marchese Freganeschi Oratore della Città di Cremona per dimonstrare che nel nuovo generale Censimento i more-gelsi debbono ser compresi nel censo (1753?).''

Miscellanea: Censo ed imposte, Nr. 3. A bound, unpaginated volume in the Biblioteca Nationale Braidenese of Milan.

Contains: Count Prass, ''Progetto d'un nuovo Sistema di Taglia da praticarsi nello Stato di Milano (1709).''

''Riflessioni del Principato di Pavia sopra il nuovo Progetto di Taglia proposto per lo Stato di Milano l'anno 1709 (n.d.).''

Untitled memorandum about Prass' ''Progetto'' by the Giunta di Governo (1712).

''Riflessioni della Città di Milano sopra i progetti del Conte di Prass, e della Città di Cremona (1710).''

Untitled reply to Prass by the province of Tortona (n.d.).

''Risposta per la Communità di Voghera al Progetto del nuovo Sistema di Taglia (n.d.).''

''Risposta della Città e Provincia di Cremona al Progetto di nuovo Sistema di Taglia (1709).''

Untitled reply to Prass by the city of Vigevano (n.d.).

Untitled reply to Prass by the province of Vigevano (n.d.).

Untitled brief by the city and province of Milan about the method of evaluating land (1726).

Untitled petition of the Congregation of State about the method of evaluating land (10 October 1726).

Untitled petition of the Congregation of State about the method of evaluating land (late 1726 or early 1727).

"Progetto d'autore anonimo fatto alla ECCma. Real Giunta del Nuovo Censimento per la riduzione di tutti le carichi regi esistenti presentemente nello Stato di Milano a un solo metodo uniforme per l'universale ripartimento, e riflessioni della ECCLLma. Congregazione del medesimo Stato in opposto fatte presenti alla stessa ECCLLma. Giunta nel entrante Maggio 1732."

Moreau de Beaumont, Jean Louis, *Memoires concernant les impositions et droits en Europe et en France*, Vol. 1. Paris: De L'imprimerie Royale, 1768.

Neri, Pompeo, "Discorso sopra lo stato antico e moderno della nobilità di Toscana (1748)," in Ioannis Bonaventurae Neri Badia, *Regiae Celsitudinis Serenissimi Magni Ducis Etruriae in signatura libellorum supplicum gratiae et iustitiae consiliarii Decisiones et responsa iuris. Tomus secondus continens eius dem responsa quibus accedunt Pompeii filii Decisiones responsa et discursus legales*. Florence, 1776.

Idem, "Memoria sulla mendicita (1767)," in *Illuministi italiani*, ed. Franco Venturi, Vol. 3. Milan: Ricciardi, 1958.

Idem, "Osservazioni sopra il prezzo legale delle monete (1751)," in *Scrittori classici italiani di economia politica, Parte antica*, ed. P. Custodi, Vol. 6. Milan: Destefanis, 1804.

Idem, Relazione dello stato in cui si trova l'opera del Censimento universale del Ducato di Milano nel mese di Maggio dell'Anno 1750. Milan: Stampatore Regio Camerale, 1750. Abbreviated as *PR*.

Idem, "Sopra la materia frumentaria (1767)," in *Scrittori classici italiani di economia politica, Parte moderna*. Vol. 49 (Supplimento). Milan: Imperiale Regia Stamperia, 1816.

Raccolta degli editti, ordini, istruzione e lettere circolare pubblicati dal Magistrato Camerale e successivi governi. Milan: Majnardi, 1802. Abbreviated as *Raccolta Magistrato Camerale*.

Raccolta degli editti, ordini, istruzione, riforme e lettere circolare istrutive della Real Giunta del Censimento Generale dello Stato di Milano, 2d ed. Milan: Majnardi, 1802. Abbreviated as *Raccolta Giunta*.

Raccolta degli editti, ordini, istruzioni e lettere circolare pubblicati dalla Regia Provisionale Delegazione del Censimento generale dello Stato di Milano, 2d ed. Milan: Majnardi, 1802. Abbreviated as *Raccolta Provisionale Delegazione*.

La riforma finanziaria nella Lombardia austriaca nel XVIII secolo, ed. C.A. Vianello. Milan: Giuffrè, 1940.

Smith, Adam, *The Wealth of Nations*, Vol. 2. Homewood (Ill.): Richard D. Irwin, 1963.

Turgot, A.R.J., *Oeuvres de Turgot*, ed. G. Schelle, Vol. 2. Paris: Alcan, 1914.

Verri, Pietro, *Carteggio di Pietro e di Alessandro Verri*, ed. E. Greppi & A. Giulini. 12 Vols. Milan: Cogliati, Milesi, Giuffrè, 1923-1942.

Idem, Lettere e scritti inediti, ed. Carlo Casati, Vol. 4. Milan: Galli, 1881.

Idem, "Meditazioni sull'economia politica (1771)," in *Del piacere a del dolore ed altre scritti di filosofia ed economia*, ed. R. Felice. Novara: Feltrinelli, 1964.

Idem, "Meditazioni sull'economia politica (with annotations by Ginarinaldo Carli)," in *Biblioteca dell'economisti*, Ser. 1, Vol. 3. Turin: Pomba, 1852.

Idem, "Meditazioni sull'economia politica con annotazioni di Gianraldo Carli," in *Scrittori classici italiani di economia politica, Parte moderna*, ed. P. Custodi, Vol. 15. Milan: Destefanis, 1804.

Idem, "Memoria cronologica dei cambiamenti pubblici dello Stato di Milano, 1750-1795 (1795?)," in *Lettere e scritti inediti*, ed. Carlo Casati, Vol. 4. Milan: Galli, 1881.

Idem, "Memorie storiche sulla economia pubblica dello Stato di Milano (1768)," in *Scrittori classici italiani di economia politica, Parte moderna*, ed. P. Custodi, Vol. 17. Milan: Destefanis, 1804.

Idem, "Sulle leggi vincolanti principal mente nel commercio de grani (1769)." in *Scrittori classici italiani di economia politica, Parte moderna*, ed. P. Custodi, Vol. 16. Milan: Destefanis, 1804.

Idem, "Sullo stato politico del Milanese nel 1790 (1790)," in *Scritti Vari*, ed. G. Carcano, Vol. 2. Florence: Monnier, 1854.

B: Secondary works.

Annoni, Ada, "Gli inizi della dominazione austriaca," in *Storia di Milano*, Vol. 12. Milan: Fondazione Treccani degli Alfieri per la storia di Milano, 1959.

Anzilotti, Antonio, "Stato e chiesa in Toscana (1911)," in *Movimenti e contrasti per l'unità italiana*, ed. A. Caracciolo. Milan: Giuffrè, 1964.

Idem, "Il tramonto dello stato citadino," *Archivio storica italiano*, Ser. 7, Vol. 1 (1924).

Beloch, Karl J., *Bevölkerungsgeschichte Italiens*, Vol. 3. Berlin: De Gruyter, 1961.

Büchi, Herman, *Finanzen und Finanzpolitik Toskanas im Zeitalter der Aufklärung.* Berlin: Matthiesen Verlag (Lübeck), 1915. (*Historische Studien, Heft* 124).

Idem: Ein Menschenalter Reformen der Toten Hand in Toskana. Berlin: Matthiesen Verlag (Lübeck), 1912. (*Historische Studien, Heft* 99).

Caizzi, Bruno, "Le classi sociali nella vita milanese," in *Storia di Milano*, Vol. 11. Milan: Fondazione Treccani degli Alfieri per la storie di Milano, 1958.

Idem, *Il Comasco sotto il dominio austriaco fino alla redazione del catasto teresiano.* Como: Centro lariano per gli studi economici, 1955.

Idem, *Il Comasco sotto il dominio spagnolo.* Como: Centro lariano per gli studi economici, 1955.

Idem, *Industria, commercio e banca in Lombardia nel XVIII secolo.* Milan: Banca Commerciale Italiana, 1968.

Candeloro, Giorgio, *Storia dell'Italia moderna*, Vol. 1. Milan: Feltrinelli, 1956.

Catalano, Franco, *Illuministi e giacobini del settecento italiano.* Milan: Istituto Editoriale Cisalpino, 1959.

Idem, "Il problema delle affittanza nella seconda metà del settecento in un'inchiesta piemontese del 1793," *Annali dell'Istituto Giangiacomo Feltrinelli*, Vol. 2 (1959).

Cattaneo, Carlo, "L'agricoltura inglese paragonata alla nostra (1857)," in

Scritti economici, ed. A. Bertolino, Vol. 3. Florence: Monnier, 1956.

Idem, "D'alcune istituzioni agrarie dell'Alta Italia applicabili a sollievo dell'Irlanda (1847)," in *Scritti economici,* ed. A. Bertolino, Vol. 3. Florence: Monnier, 1956.

Idem, "Notizie naturali e civili su la Lombardia (1844)," in *Scritti storici e geografici,* ed. G. Salvemini & E. Sestan, Vol. 1. Florence: Monnier, 1957.

Idem, "Sulla legge comunale e provinciale (1864)," in *Scritti politici,* ed. M. Boneschi, Vol. 4. Florence: Monnier, 1965.

Conigliani, Carlo Angelo, *G.B. Fraganeschi e le questioni tributaria in Lombardia nel secolo XVIII.* Modena, 1898.

Dal Pane, Luigi, *La finanza toscana dagli inizi del secolo XVIII alla caduta del granducato.* Milan: Banca Commerciale Italiana, 1965.

Idem, La questione del commercio dei grani nel settecento in Italia. Milan: Cotignola, 1932.

De Stefano, Francesco, *G.R. Carli.* Modena: Societa Tipografica Modenese, 1942.

Idem, "G.R. Carli e il consiglio supremo dell'economia a Milano," *Rivista storica italina,* Ser. 4, Vol. 4 (1933).

Diaz, Furio, *Francesco Maria Gianni.* Milan-Naples: Ricciardi, 1966.

Gerschenkron, Alexander, *Continuity in History and Other Essays.* Cambridge (Mass.): Harvard University, 1968.

Idem, Economic Backwardness in Historical Prespective. Cambridge (Mass.): Harvard University, 1962.

Hall, Thadd E., "Thought and Practice of Enlightened Government in French Corsica," *American Historical Review,* Vol. 74 (1969).

Lhèritier, Michael, "Rapport génerál: le despotisme éclairé de Frederic II à la révolution française," *Bulletin of the International Committee of Historical Sciences,* Vol. 9 (Nr. 35, 1937).

Litchfield, B., "Office-holding in Florence after the Republic," in *Renaissance: Studies in Honor of Hans Baron,* ed. A. Molho & J. Tedeschi. Florence: Sansoni, 1971.

Marion, Marcel, *Historire financière de la France depuis 1715.* 4 Vols. Paris: Rousseau, 1914-1925.

Idem, Les impôts directs sous l'ancien régime. Paris: É. Cornély, 1910.

Masetti-Bencini, I., "Notizie su Pompeo Neri e su alcuni suoi scritti," *Miscellanea storica della Valdelsa,* Vol. 22 (1914).

May, Louis Philippe, "Despotisme légal et despotisme éclairé d'après Le Mercier de la Rivière," *Bulletin of the International Committee of Historical Sciences,* Vol. 9 (Nr. 34, 1937).

Mirri, Mario, "Un inchiesta toscana sui tributi pagati dai mezzadri e sui patti colonici nella seconda metà del settecento," *Annali dell'Istituto Giangiacomo Feltrinelli,* Vol. 2 (1959).

Idem, "Proprietari e contadini toscani nelle riforme leopoldine," *Movimento operaio,* Vol. 7 (1955).

Idem, "Sallustio Antonio Bandini," in *Dizionario biografico degli Italiani,* Vol. 5. Rome: Istituto della Enciclopedia Italiana, 1963.

Morandi, Carlo, *Idee e formazione politiche in Lombardia dal 1748 al 1814.* Turin: Fratelli Bocca, 1927.

Mori, Renato, *"Il movimento reazionario in Toscana alle riforme economiche leopoldine nel 1790,'' Archivio storico italiano,* Vol. 100 (1942).

Nuccio, Oscar, Biographic essay on Neri, in Pompeo Neri, "Documenti anessi alle Osservazione sopra il prezzo legale delle monete," *Scrittori classici italiani di economia politica, Parte antica,* Vol. 7. Milan: Destefanis, 1804; reprint ed. Rome: Bizzari, 1965.

Pugliese, S., "Condizione economiche e finanziarie della Lombardia nella prima metà del secolo XVIII," in *Miscellanea di storia italiani,* Ser. 3, Vol. 21. Turin: Bocca, 1924.

Ricca Salerno, Giuseppe, *Storia delle dottrini finanziarie in Italia.* Palermo: Alberto Reber, 1896.

Rocchi, Gaetano, "Pompeo Neri," *Archivio storico italiano,* Ser. 3, Vol. 24 (1876).

Romani, Mario, *L'agricoltura in Lombardia dal periodo delle riforme al 1859.* Milan: Società Editrice "Vita e Pensiero", 1957.

Idem, "L'agricoltura lodigiana e la 'nuova agricoltura' del settecento," *Archivio storico lombardo,* Ser. 8, Vol. 8 (1958).

Idem, "L'economia milanese nel settecento," in *Storia di Milano,* Vol. 12. Milan: Fondazione Treccani degli Alfieri per la storia di Milano, 1959.

Romeo, Rosario, *Risorgimento e capitalismo.* Bari: Laterza, 1963.

Rota, Ettore, *L'Austria in Lombardia e la preparazione del movimento democratico cisalpino.* Rome-Milan-Naples: Società Editrice Dante Alighieri, 1911.

Sebastiani, Lucia, *La tassazione degli ecclesiastici nella Lombardia teresiana, con una memoria di Pompeo Neri.* Milan-Rome-Naples-Città di Castello: Società Editrice Dante Alighieri, 1969.

Sereni, Emilio, *Storia del paesaggio agrario italiano.* Bari: Laterza, 1962.

Storia di Milano, Vols. 11-12. Milan: Fondazione Treccani degli Alfieri per la storia di Milano, 1958-1959.

Stourm, Rene, *Les finances de l'ancien régime et de la révolution,* Vol. 1. Paris: Guillaumin, 1885.

Tosi, Dario, "Sulle forme iniziali di sviluppo economico e i loro effetti nel lungo periodo: l'agricoltura italiana e l'accumulazione capitalistica" *Annali dell'Istituto Giangiacomo Feltrinelli,* Vol. 4 (1961).

Tozzi, Glauco, "Salustio Bandini, economista senese," in *Memoria della R. Accademia Nazionale dei Lincei, classe di scienza, morali, storiche e filologiche,* Ser. 6, Vol. 5. Rome: Accademia Nazionale dei Lincei, 1933.

Valeri, Nino, *Pietro Verri.* Milan: Mondadori, 1937.

Valsecchi, Franco, *L'assolutismo illuminato in Austria e in Lombardia,* Vol. 2, Part 1. Bologna: Zanichelli, 1934.

Idem, "Dalla pace di Aquisgrana alla battaglia di Lodi," in *Storia di Milano,* Vol. 12. Milan: Fondazione Treccani degli Alfieri per la storia di Milano, 1959.

Idem, L'Italia nel seicento e nel settecento. Turin: Tipografia Sociale Torinese, 1967.

Venturi, Franco, Biographic essays on Sallustio Bandini, Pompeo Neri and Gianrinaldo Carli, in *Illuministi italiani,* ed. Franco Venturi, Vol. 3., Milan: Ricciardi, 1958.

Idem, Settecento riformatore. Turin: Einaudi, 1969.

Idem, Utopia and Reform in the Enlightenment. Cambridge (Eng.): Cambridge University, 1971.

Verga, Ettore, *I consigli del comune di Milano*, n. p., n. d.

Vianello, C.A., *Il settecento milanese*. Milan: Baldini & Castoldi, 1934.

Villani, Rosario, *Mezzogiorno e contadini nell'età moderna*. Bari: Laterza, 1961.

Vismara, Gulio, "Le istituzioni del patriziato," in *Storia di Milano*, Vol. 11. Milan: Fondazione Treccani degli Alfieri per la storia di Milano, 1958.

Vivanti, Corrado, *Le campagne mantovano nell'età delle riforme*. Milan: Feltrinelli, 1959.

Wandruszka, Adam, *Leopold II*, 2 Vols. Vienna: Herold, 1965.

Weulersse, Georges, *Le mouvement physiocratique en France*, Vol. 1. Paris: Alcan, 1910.

Zangheri, Renato, *La proprietà terriera e le origini del Risorgimento nel Bolognese*. Bologna: Zanichelli, 1961.

Zaninelli, Sergio, *Una grande azienda agricola della pianura irrigua lombardia nei secoli XVIII e XIX*. Milan: Giuffrè, 1964.

Idem, *Il nuovo censo dello Stato di Milano dall'editto del 1718 al 1733*. Milan: Società Editrice "Vita e Pensiero", 1963.

Idem, "Un 'Progetto d'un nuovo sistema di taglia da praticarsi nello Stato di Milano' del 1709," *Archivio storico lombardo*, Ser. 8, Vol. 10 (1960).

Ziliotto, Baccio, 'Primi moti antioligarchi a Capodistria," *Archivio Veneto*, Ser. 5, Vols. 54-55 (1954).

INDEX

Abiate-Grasso, 60
Bandini, Sallustio, 29-31, 32
Bank of Santo Ambrogio, 13, 59
Beccaria, Cesare, 2
Boisguillebert, Pierre Le Pesant de, 29-30
Bologna, 14-15
Cameral Magistracy, 73-75, 78
Canzo, 60
Capodistria, 67-69, 76, 78
Cardano, 79-80
Carli, Gianrinaldo, praises Censimento, 1; his "Relazione del Censimento," 24; on evaluations, 35-37; on communal government, 50; on chancellors, 53; on metropolitan government, 55; leadership of Economic Council, chapter V
Carpani, Francesco, 55, 66, 73
Casal Maggiore, 19, 20, 21, 40, 57-58, 81
Castel-Leone, 62
Castelli, Giuliano, 73
Cattaneo, Carlo, 1, 35, 48, 50
Cavalry tax, 11, 22, 40
Chancellor, 51, 52-54, 63-64, 78, 80
Charles VI, Emperor, 8, 17, 22
Cisalpine Republic, 15
Commercial deputy, 48, 50-51, 60, 75
Commercial farmers, 4, 17, 34
Commercial tax, 19, 33-35, 50-51, 66
Common lands, 50, 52, 78-80, 82
Como, 15, 22, 58
Concordat of 1757, 9-10, 37-39
Congregation of State views of Censimento, 1, 14; organization of, 6, 57-59; on evaluations, 15-

17; on mulberry enumeration, 18-19; on personal tax and unified administration, 20-22; on church exemption, 38; Neri's views of, 63; Verri's views of, 64, 73; Carli's views of, 71
Conigliani, Carlo Angelo, 41, 43
Corn cultivation, 4, 37
Council General of Milan, 6, 14, 55-56, 58-59, 64, 71-72
Council of 60, see Council General of Milan
Cremona and Prass, 7-8; on evaluations, 15; on mulberry enumeration, 19; on personal tax, 20-21; and joint reply, 40, 81; and Freganeschi, 41-42; on reform, 43; reform of, 57, 62, 64
Cristiani, Bltrame, 24, 37-38
Dandolo, Vincenzo, 35, 82
Diaria, 6-8, 11, 22
Ducato, 15, 18, 36, 39-40, 42-43, 58-59
Eugene of Savoy, 6, 8
Exactor, 4, 13-14, 45-46, 49-50, 52, 74-75
Exemptions, 7-8, 9-10, 37-39
Feudal institutions, 3, 4, 26, 32, 52
Firmian, Carlo Gottardo, 41, 54, 63, 73
Florence, 25, 27-29, 32
Foebonnais, Francois Veron de, 1, 35
France, 1-2, 7, 9, 14, 30
Freganeschi, Giambattista, 36, 41-44, 81
Gravedona, 62
Gravisi, Girolamo, 68-69
Gravisi, Giuseppe, 67-69
Greppi, Antonio, 72-73
Indirect taxation, 66, 73
International Committee of Historical Sciences, 2

Joseph II, 63-64, 78, 81
Kaunitz-Rittberg, Count, 63, 71, 77-78
Lodi, 16, 20, 40, 57-59, 81
Lottinger, Stefano, 73
Lupi, Carlo, 17
Mantua, 46
Maremma, 29-30
Maria Theresa, 24, 40, 50, 53, 67, 78-79
Marion, Marcel, 7
Medici, Cosimo, 25
Medici, Ferdinando, 25
Medici, Gian Castone, 25
Mensuale, 5-8, 10-11, 12
Mercimonio, see Commercial tax
Milan, patriciate, 4; tax advantages, 5, 13; on Prass, 6-7; and Miro Commission, 14-15, 18-19, 20, 22; and Commercial tax, 33; and Provisional Commission, 38; and Ducato, as center of opposition, 43-44; reform of, 55, 58-59, 64; and Supreme Economic Council, 66, 71-73, 77
Miro, Vincenzo foreigness, 2; appointment, 9; strategies, 10, 13-4; death, 11; on evaluations, 15-17; on mulberry enumeration, 18-19; on personal tax, 21; legacy, 24
Montorfani, Giovanni, 42
Monza, 60
Moreau de Beaumont, Jean Louis, 1
Naples, 46
Neri, Giovanno Bonaventura, 25
Neri, Giovanni Iacopo, 25
Neri, Pompeo and Progress Report, 1; foreigness, 2; on old tax, 6, 12-13; on Miro Commission, 9; on exemptions, 10, 37-39; and opposition, 14, 81; and evaluations, 15-16, 34-35, 38; on mulberry enumeration, 18; on personal tax, 21, 34; on unified administration, 23; life and work in Tuscany, chapter II; leadership of Second Commission, 33, 40; dismissal, 38; and local government, 45-46, 49, 52, 53, 56, 61-62; and common lands, 50; on Congregation of State, 63; and Verri, 64-65; and Carli, 67, 71
Novara, 15, 20-21
Nuovo metodo per le scuole pubbliche di Italia, 70
Pallavicini, Gianluca, 24-25
Pavia on Prass, 7-8, 13; on personal tax, 20-21; on unified administration, 23; and joint reply, 40, 81; reform of, 55, 57, 59
Perlongo, Count, 9
Personal deputy, 48-51, 60, 75, 80
Personal tax, 5, 19-22, 33-35, 41-42, 50-51, 74
Peter Leopold, Grand Duke and Emperor, 12, 14, 25-26, 28-29, 30, 63
Physiocrats, 14
Prass, Count, 6-8, 43
Progetto d'un nuovo sustema di taglia, 6-7
Progress Report, and France, 1; on the old tax, 6, 12-13, 24; on the Miro Commission, 9; on opposition, 13-14, 32; on the state, 25-26; on civil nobility, 28, 45; on evaluations, 35; response to, 39, 42, 81; on Congregation of State, 63
Property deputy establishment of and duties, 47-51; and chancellors, 53-54; and metropolitan government, 55, 57-58; and large communes, 60-62; and Verri, 64; and enforcement, 74-75; in Cardano, 80
Provincial deputy, 54-59, 70
Provisional Commission, 38-39, 66
Rice, 4, 17, 76
Roman law, 1, 25, 31
Romani, Mario, 20
Salt tax, 11, 22
Senate of Milan, 8, 67, 71-73
Sericulture, 4, 10, 17-19, 35-37, 42-43
Smith, Adam, 1
Soresina, 62
Supreme Economic Council, 66, 71, 73, 75-76, 800

Tortona, 8, 19, 20-21
Triviglio, 60-62
Turgot, A.R.J., 14
Tuscany, 12, 14, 25, 26-32, 62
l'Uomo libero, 69-70, 77
Valsecchi, Franco, 2, 40
Varese, 60-62, 79
Vauban, Sebastian Le Prestre, 7
Venetian Republic, 67-69
Venturi, Franco, 32, 77
Verri, Gabriele, 20
Vjri, Pietro foreigness, 2; on
   Freganeschi, 41; on local
   government, 50; on chancellors,
   53; on metropolitan government,
   55; constitutional proposal, 63-
   65; on Austrian rule, 72-73, 81;
   political economyof, 76, 78;
   optimism of, 77; and Neri, 81
Vianello, C.A., 35
Vicario of Provision, 14, 58-59, 71-
   72
Vigevano, 8, 15, 19
Voghera, 8
Zaninelli, Sergio, 9